Harvester New Readings

This established paperback series offers a range of important new critical introductions to English writers, responsive to new bearings which have recently emerged in literary analysis. Its aim is to make more widely current and available the perspectives of contemporary literary theory, by applying these to a selection of the most widely read and studied English authors.

The range of issues covered varies with each author under survey. The series as a whole resists the adoption of general theoretical principles, in favour of the candid and original application of the critical and theoretical models found most appropriate to the survey of each individual author. The series resists the representation of any single either traditionally or radically dominant discourse, working rather with the complex of issues which emerge from a close and widely informed reading of the author in question in his or her social, political and historical context.

The perspectives offered by these lucid and accessible introductory books should be invaluable to students seeking an understanding of the full range and complexity of the concerns of key canonical writers. The major concerns of each author are critically examined and sympathetically and lucidly reassessed, providing indispensable handbooks to the work of major English authors seen from new perspectives.

David Aers	*Chaucer*
James Booth	*Larkin*
Joseph Bristow	*Robert Browning*
Angus Calder	*T. S. Eliot*
Brian Cummings	*Donne*
Steve Davies	*Milton*
Alexander Davis	*Ted Hughes*
Simon Dentith	*George Eliot*
Kate Flint	*Dickens*
Paul Hamilton	*Wordsworth*
Brean Hammond	*Pope*
Bernard O'Donoghue	*Heaney*
Adrian Poole	*Henry James*
Kiernan Ryan	*Shakespeare*
Simon Shepherd	*Spenser*
Nigel Wood	*Swift*

Short
Loan

HARVESTER
New Readings

Robert Browning

Joseph Bristow

Lecturer in English Literature
at the University of York

HARVESTER WHEATSHEAF

New York   London   Toronto   Sydney   Tokyo   Singapore

First published 1991 by
Harvester Wheatsheaf
66 Wood Lane End, Hemel Hempstead
Hertfordshire HP2 4RG
A division of
Simon & Schuster International Group

Typeset in 11/13pt Goudy Old Style
by Keyboard Services, Luton
Printed and bound in Great Britain by
Billing and Sons Ltd, Worcester

British Library Cataloguing in Publication Data

Bristow, Joseph
    Robert Browning. – (Harvester new readings)
    I. Title   II. Series
    821

    ISBN 0–7450–0733–3
    ISBN 0–7450–0734–1 pbk

1 2 3 4 5   95 94 93 92 91

Contents

Preface

Robert Browning would have liked his poetry to have been read anew – at least in theory. For he himself was a radical rereader. The revisionary impulse in his writing is very strong indeed. His restless, ambitious and often extraordinarily difficult work self-consciously impresses its distinctive mark on received poetic traditions. With these points in mind, one of his finest modern critics has argued that, in several related senses, Browning wrote a 'poetry of the future'.[1] It is a richly suggestive phrase. To a large degree Browning's extensive corpus of poems and plays is certainly structured on a principle of 'futurity' or 'disclosure': they resist endings, constantly seeking new beginnings, eagerly anticipating events to come. His style – especially his often fractured, lengthy and contorted syntax – deploys complex techniques of deferral and delay. It produces highly discursive, if not insistently garrulous, writing forever heading towards some as yet unrealised goal.

This unique style, however, is not the only aspect of his forward looking address to the 'future'. He was the Victorian poet most fully (even if reluctantly) absorbed by his Modernist heirs. His innovative use of the dramatic persona, and his development of the monologue, may make him appear exceptionally avant-garde. But he is likely not to have agreed with the manner in which his own work was revised, or with the many fascinating readings brought to bear upon his poems in the twentieth century. He had his own ideas about renewal, and these were, at times, inflexible.

It should go without saying that Browning – if charged with ever expectant energies, presaging drastic shifts in modern poetry – was understandably very much a man of his time. His zealous concern with transforming past materials into modern ones is encompassed by a sometimes prescriptive religious aesthetic that emerged from radical dissenting elements of the Victorian middle classes. To read the world with new eyes – as he sought to – meant to perform God's duty. And he undertook this demanding, if not impossible, task in a society that was becoming more and more secular. This book examines why he laboured so hard in poetry to implement ideas about the divine necessity of cultural change, and the peculiar scepticism, historical paradoxes, and strange negativities this makes for in his writing. The aesthetic, political and stylistic models to which he adhered are remarkably consistent across the main part of his career. Although committed to an active principle of cultural progress, Browning had arrived at his understanding of it early in life, and it was one that forced remarkably few alterations on his writing thereafter. His work as a poet is marked more by modifications, rather than decisive breaks, in his system of belief. His religious faith, above all, remained unsullied, and it circumscribed his understanding of what could and could not be entertained within God's plan of human development. In other words, only certain changes could be explored and explained in his poetry, since a rationale of divine inspiration underwrote his every word. Having such a clear idea of what poetry had to renew enabled him to compose at length and with regularity. Consequently, his work often has to negotiate the tensions that result from a belief, on the one hand, in the necessity of shifts and breaks in historical and cultural consciousness with, on the other, an unswerving commitment to the divine motives that put this chain of events into motion in the first place. At its simplest, the main problem he had to confront and resolve concerned whether human individuals made their own history for themselves or had it made for them by an altogether higher power.

The readings offered in this study are necessarily selective, given the vast number of works he published between 1833 and 1889. But it aims overall to provide a representative account of the main features of his writing. It also draws on a large body of research, pointing readers in the direction of other relevant modern critical works. Wherever possible, links have been forged between Browning's poetry and its Victorian cultural contexts. Most of the discussion concentrates on his better known poems. At points, connections are made with comparatively neglected works, particularly those he published after The Ring and the Book (1868–9). Chapters focus on his most pronounced preoccupations – his position as a post-Romantic writer; his use of the dramatic monologue; his theory of history and engagement with mid-nineteenth-century debates about historicism; and his representation of love, sex, and marriage – all of which are bounded by his unwavering view that each of these concerns is also God's, and which he, as a poet, has the privilege to explain. But this privilege is problematically shot through with a strangely confident perplexity, since it is also his obligation, as a poet, to declare that he cannot fully know the infinite wisdom which has brought his work into being, and which may only partly glimmer within the finite form of that limited, unwieldy tool – language. Yet language, for all its deficiencies, must inevitably serve as his sole intermediary between finite and infinite realms. So all he can do, he claims, is to try to fashion the seemingly intractable materiality of language into poetry to commune with the greatest Maker of them all. Beneath this burden, he must continually fail, and yet he is compelled to seek to overcome that failure by acknowledging that the task set before him is an almost insurmountable but urgent one. For poetry, he believes, is obliged to bear witness to processes of renewal that God installed in the first place, and which poetry – from one age to another – must strive to comprehend. It is this particular point that makes Browning's work strenuously self-reflexive, stylistically difficult, and – in that – absorbing in its restlessness. Little wonder he was considered, particularly towards the end of his life, as a kind of priest, prophet or sage for intellectually troubled Victorian times.

Quotations have been taken from the Penguin edition of Browning's poems edited by John Pettigrew with Thomas J. Collins (1981) and the Penguin edition of *The Ring and the Book* edited by Richard D. Altick (1971). These are reliable texts. Both editions contain a wealth of helpful explanatory notes. Pettigrew and Collins include suggestions for additional critical reading. Their two volumes of *The Poems* follow the collected *Poetical Works* published in 1888–9 that Browning saw through the press in the months immediately leading up to his death. Most of his work from 1833 through to the 1880s was subject to revision, some of it very considerable indeed, and editors continue to dispute whether the first or final versions should stand as their copy text. Altick reprints the first edition of *The Ring and the Book*, arguing that the 1889 revisions often 'left the text worse off'.[2] It has to be said that, until recently, the whole question of editing Browning's poetry was in a parlous state. The Ohio variorum edition was subjected to severe criticisms when it was first published in 1969 (be wary: some of the errors contained in the first four volumes are truly startling). Ohio University Press has tried to remedy this situation, continuing its potentially valuable project under prudently tightened editorial procedures. At the time of writing, four volumes of the Oxford University Press edition, under the general editorship of Ian Jack, have been published. Annotations to this edition are meticulous and are enhanced by fulsome cross-references and allusions to many of Browning's more obscurantist interests (the poet was a self-taught, and extremely unsystematic, scholar). The Longman Annotated Browning, edited by Daniel Karlin and John Woolford, is currently awaited, and promises to take a different direction by printing the poems in their first published form. There is, for example, a strong argument to make for taking the 1840 version of *Sordello* as a copy text, rather than the 1863 or later ones, since the original oddities of this poem have to be understood in order to grasp how and why its earliest (and often erudite) readers were confounded by it.

Some of the arguments laid out here were first developed during doctoral research at the University of Southampton under the close supervision of Isobel Armstrong. Elinor Shaffer and Robert Young gave helpful responses to that stage of my work. Two colleagues at Sheffield City Polytechnic, Rosemary Betterton and Frances Dann, introduced me to secondary materials I would not otherwise have found. Druuske Hawkridge and Derek Sharrock, graduate students of the MA in literature (Victorian poetry) at the Open University, shared a number of invaluable references with me. My thanks to them, and to the inter-library loan service at the Mary Badland Library, which delivered virtually all the remaining materials I needed to complete this book.

1

Reading Browning

In E. F. Benson's humorous reminiscences of Victorian life and letters, *As We Were* (1930), he recalls the time when Robert Browning met members of his distinguished family. This event, greeted with eager anticipation by Benson's mother and sisters, took place in 1887. Now well into his seventies, with an enthusiastic literary society established in his name, the poet was at the height of his career. Browning ranked as a major celebrity, an affable man who enjoyed wining and dining. Like all good story-tellers, Benson, one of the Archbishop of Canterbury's sons, exaggerates his tale to great effect:

> He came to dine one night with my parents in London: if the family had been allowed to commandeer the presence of whom they would, as guest, the vote would probably have been cast for him, for not only was my mother an ardent Browningite, but one of her daughters knew really prodigious quantities of his work by heart, and was willing, if anyone doubted it, to go on repeating his poems till there could be no question about her claim; while one of the boys, a year or two before, had devoted the money for a prize he won in some athletic competition at school to the purchase of

1

the six volumed edition of his work, instead of buying a silver cup with his own name enwreathed in *repoussé* ferns. The guest was immensely genial, he ate and drank and talked with a juvenile pleasure, as if the world held many joyful surprises for him still. Then one of these pert creatures asked him what he thought of Austin Dobson as a poet, for there were strong differences of opinion in the family about him. He laughed, sipped his port, and then he said, 'Well, some people do like carved cherrystones'. His audience approved of that, for they found it characteristic of one who in his entrancing 'Men and Women' [1855] told you with huge gusto not what he thought, but what fifty other people thought, and did not say a word on his own account till the last poem of all. Just such a word he said on his own account that evening quite at the end of dinner, and it is for that reason I am telling the story, since to this day it stands in greater need of interpretation than anything he wrote.[1]

This amusingly condescending account is significant in several respects. Not only does it mock the notorious obscurity of Browning's poetry, which gave rise to the various *Handbooks* devised to interpret his works, and provoked plenty of complaints from his earliest readers; it also lays an emphasis on Browning's surprisingly ingenuous behaviour, which hardly squares with the frequent abstruseness of his poetry. Moreover, Benson's remarks indicate how important the poet's dramatic monologues in *Men and Women* had become, suggesting that there is something oddly evasive about Browning's well known use of the poetic persona. These are, indeed, the main things about Browning's poetry that have preoccupied Victorian and modern criticism. Eccentric, difficult, perverse even, Browning also seems rather childlike – as if he were blithely unaware of his stylistic obscurity. He is hardly the sophisticated raconteur that the upper-class Benson might have expected. Instead, he is a source of light entertainment for the ladies who were, we are led to believe, naively entranced by a poet optimistically pursuing the hidden truths of the world. Benson was not alone in poking fun at Browning in this way. His snobbish caricature leaves an impression about the poet shared by many other commentators.

Another late Victorian, Oscar Wilde, also poured scorn on Browning's poetry, if with altogether different intentions in mind. For Wilde admired, but none the less could see the faults of, the poet's highly individualistic manner of expression. Here, in *The Critic as Artist* (1890, 1891), Wilde's aesthete, Gilbert, laughably makes Browning's every verbal vice into a sort of virtue:

> Rhyme, that exquisite echo which is the Muse's hollow hill creates and answers its own voice . . . became in Robert Browning's hands a grotesque, misshapen thing . . . Yet, he was great: and though he turned language into ignoble clay, he made from it men and women that live . . . Even now, as I am speaking, and speaking not against but for him, there glides through the room the pageant of his persons . . . Yes, Browning was great, and as what will he be remembered? As a poet? Ah, not as a poet! He will be remembered as a writer of fiction, as the most supreme writer of fiction, it may be that we ever had . . . The only man who can touch the hem of his garment is George Meredith. Meredith is a prose Browning, and so is Browning. He used poetry as a medium for writing in prose.[2]

Since Browning radically shifted the boundaries of poetry, wilfully violating its rules of decorum, Wilde obviously finds his work a great source of comedy. But, unlike Benson, Wilde makes the joke almost entirely in Browning's favour. Wilde always held an idiosyncratic style in high regard when it challenged orthodoxies. Wilde states that Browning, whether by aim or default, produced 'grotesque' art with abundant energy, and that is its merit. Zealous, prolific and consistently demanding, Browning always communicated a sense of urgency in his poetry. Between them Benson and Wilde provide a reasonably good sense of Browning's place in cultural memory, as a mild-mannered Victorian who wrote some crucially important but peculiarly indigestible poems. Biographers have at times probed, and found themselves unable to answer, the seeming incongruity between the poet's sympathetic personality (he was socially well liked) and the often compacted nature of his poems (hosts of reviewers claimed he was unreadable).

Many other myths circulate around the life of Browning. To begin with he is mostly remembered for his extraordinary courtship with Elizabeth Barrett between 1844 and 1846, and the amazing correspondence it produced. The present study does not analyse in detail that remarkable body of material, which has much to say about his views on poetry and poets. The Brownings' love letters, which comment amply on Mr Barrett's tyrannous behaviour, their secret marriage in Marylebone Church, and their escape to Italy, were a *cause célèbre* when published in 1894. A stage play, and then a film, in 1931, would follow, and so a powerful and truly enchanting love story would come to surround these married partners in poetry. Set up as an ideal couple who held a singularly romantic view of the world, they are unlikely to appear as liberal individualists whose work maps out a great many crises in bourgeois self-identity. Their marriage, in any case, was based on rather different principles from that of most Victorians.

A rather wry analysis of their relationship is lightly (if very thoughtfully) sketched by Virginia Woolf in *Flush* (1922), which views the lovers from the point of view of Barrett Browning's pet spaniel. By writing the life of her dog, rather than Barrett Browning herself, Woolf was lightly sending up the way in which biography constructs its subject, wittily undermining the all too cosy accounts of the Brownings to be found on library shelves. Perhaps to see Browning from a dog's point of view is just as valid any other? Browning may well have agreed, since his work often looks at other people's lives from oblique angles. As Benson notes, Browning's writing appears to point away from the poet, making it all the more difficult to estimate the relation between the man and his work. All that needs to be said here is that Browning himself was acutely aware of any potential confusion between himself and the men and women of his imagination. He wrote in an age when the poetic voice was often read in autobiographical terms, and he did his utmost to extricate one from the other. His personae, he insisted, were not him: 'so many utterances of so many imaginary persons, not mine', as he noted in the advertisement to *Dramatic Lyrics* (1842). This shift of emphasis – from person to persona – marks one of the most significant changes Browning accomplished in the course of nineteenth-century poetry. He was the chief Victorian exponent of the dramatic monologue, although he never applied that generic definition to his work. The monologue, however, was certainly not the only form he developed during his long and finally successful career.

As with all canonical authors, a great deal of highly special-ised scholarship attends almost every formal and aesthetic question arising from his work. His considerable legacy reson-ates throughout literary modernism, with its interest in a poetics of impersonality. W. B. Yeats, in his adoption of the 'mask'; T. S. Eliot, in his frequent use of the persona; and Pound, most importantly of all, in his early collection, tellingly named *Personae* (1909): each poet's writing, either directly or indirect-ly, bears the traces of Browning's psychological exploration of the monologue. Pound is indeed Browning's rightful (if often resistant) heir, and the connections between the two offer a fertile area of inquiry.[3] Yet in his own time, between the pub-lication of his first collection in 1833 and his last in 1889, Browning's progress as a poet followed a very uneven pattern. He was barely known as a writer of any significance until the publication of his *magnum opus*, *The Ring and the Book*, in 1868–9. In fact, for sixteen years he wrote and published in the shadow of Elizabeth Barrett Browning. With her *Poems* of 1844, Barrett (before she had taken Browning's surname) gained a popularity enjoyed by no woman before. She was older, far more established, and just as well educated as her future husband. He, in the meantime, had already produced a large and varied amount of poetry and drama, known only to select circles such as the Pre-Raphaelite brotherhood and their associates. For at least the first two decades of his adult life, Browning saw himself as a misunderstood artist. Time and again he received an inauspicious reception from a literary establishment affronted by his predominantly idiosyncratic style. Until 1855 at least he kept devising differing formats for his work, in a vain effort to win an audience. He saw poetry as his vocation, and managed to keep writing and to turn his hand to no other work, with the generous support of his parents. It is true to say that he made a life out of poetry, eventually accruing a reasonable income from it. This was an unusual achievement, even in his own time.

A particular configuration of events changed Browning's fortunes in the 1860s. After Barrett Browning's death in 1861 he returned to England to become more prolific than ever before. By the 1870s, as his bibliography shows, he was composing a volume of poetry practically every other year. They sold very well, having initial print runs of several thousands. And yet, by this time, it was for some of his earlier work that he was gaining increasing admiration. Hardly any of Browning's writing produced in the last two decades of his life is, rightly or wrongly, presently regarded of much worth. Many of these later poems are long narratives, and may be classed as verse-novels. There has been a marked absence of substantial modern criticism concerning this part of his oeuvre. One of the paradoxes of Browning's rise to fame is that his two volumes of monologues, *Men and Women* and *Dramatis Personae* (1864), would not be widely appreciated until many years after their publication. When English literature began to be taught in universities at the end of the century, the process of canonization meant that much of his later writing (from the 1870s and 1880s) was dismissed as less valuable than these two collections. It would seem that longer works, such as *Red Cotton Night-Cap Country* (1873), have been counted out of Browning's 'major' writings because they are simply too discursive (and they are often exceptionally long-winded). The same might be said of his dramas and his ambitious – and most truly original – poem, *Sordello*, which he tried on two occasions to make more intelligible to a bewildered public.

All in all this means that the Browning we tend to read today roughly comprises about a third of his total output, and mostly concentrates on his innovative handling of the dramatic monologue. His early dramas (some of which reached the stage) have largely been viewed as aberrations; the long, early narratives, *Pauline* (1833), *Paracelsus* (1835) and *Sordello* bear witness, in their increasing complexity, to the considerable ambitions of a poet in his twenties, and are sometimes treated as curiosities; and his wide variety of later poems (from 1871–1889), which include experiments with new forms (such as the 'idyl'), has appeared implicitly irrelevant to his supposedly central writing. Reading Browning, therefore, is for most students and teachers a highly selective process, and even then the critical focus is frequently on form, rather than the broader cultural issues arising from each and every textual element. If, for example, the monologue has proved to be the main topic of discussion, it has far less often been understood as a form that represents political and sexual sides of that expansive and far from unified thing, the Victorian mind.

The present study mostly takes up the largely familiar and canonical Browning with one practical consideration in view: to make cultural sense of those poems that are generally taught on English literature syllabuses. The chapter divisions try to place prominent aspects of his work into convenient categories. Yet it should be clear that the poems in question are not easily contained under any one heading. No single Browning – textual, biographical or both – could or should emerge from these pages. The new readings offered here are hardly definitive.

But they try to sketch in a picture of an indefatigable poet in action, one notable for his determined sense of the need to create poems. Since the creative thrust in Browning's work is so strongly marked it actually becomes one of the key themes of his writing. A great many of his poems concern the meaning and making of poetry itself, and it is tempting to read a large part of his considerable canon as expressly involved in a project to write a poetry of poetry. It is this tendency to make poems about poems that links many areas of the present discussion. Whether he was writing about divine inspiration, the Italian Renaissance, or sexual love (and these are his main themes), Browning more often than not returns to the process which has brought his words into being. For him, as his work all too clearly indicates, this is no easy matter, since poetry is produced out of a creative struggle with obstacles that can never be completely surmounted. One of these obstacles is, in fact, poetry itself: the very material which Browning feels compelled to tell the world is inevitably inadequate to his needs. This was a point he established for himself early on in his career. How and why did he reach this seemingly self-defeating conclusion?

This question can, in part, be answered by considering Browning a post-Romantic – a modern category that helps to locate an epistemological break between literary writing produced between approximately 1770 and 1830 (the period of English Romanticism) and works published in the changing political climate of the 1830s (such as Tennyson's and Browning's). Romantic, like Victorian, only came to be used as an adjective in the 1870s, and it carries with it a great many problems of definition concerning both periodisation and aesthetic and political questions. For all its arbitrariness, Romanticism none the less points to an intense period of cultural innovation that was sorely missed by poets beginning their careers during the first decade of Victoria's reign. Born in 1812 Browning grew up in a London suburb knowing himself as neither Romantic nor Victorian but as an early nineteenth-century person. That said, as a young poet he perceived that his generation was placed at the tail end of a vital and quickly vanishing cultural moment. Literary Romanticism passed away, in effect, with the successive deaths of John Keats (1821), Percy Bysshe Shelley (1822), George Gordon Byron (1824), Samuel Taylor Coleridge (1834), and with the decline of William Wordsworth (thought by many to have lost his visionary powers when he was elected Poet Laureate in 1843). In his teens Browning was obsessed with Shelley, aghast at his idol's untimely death. Like many of his peers (notably the circle around Tennyson), he was shocked at the neglect of Keats in the 1810s. As a well read member of the middle classes he knew his Byron (*Fifine at the Fair* (1872) supplies a Victorian answer to *Don Juan* (1819)). Coleridge's influential writings on German philosophy (notably Kant) were available to him both in individual volumes and in debates within the increasingly influential periodical press. And, like radicals before and after him, he was deeply disappointed when Wordsworth, transformed in his political convictions (radical to conservative), took a minor civil service post as a tax-collector in Westmorland. For that, an act which for many aspiring writers amounted to deserting the cause of poetry, Browning penned the spirited and accusatory 'The Lost Leader' (1845). Browning's poetry is saturated with both obvious and cryptic references to the Romantic poets who were a staple part of his reading. Given their high-minded idealism, their critical response to a period of social tumult and subsequent repression, and the revolutions they accomplished in poetic form, the Romantics – in all their political divergency – must have seemed irreplaceable. This was a general feeling in literary circles during the 1820s, as this extract from a periodical article points out:

> We have lived in an age of poetry, – probably survived it. Of the *men*, some indeed remain, but the *poets*, where are they? Some are dead and some *are gone into captivity*, – 'they have hanged their

harps upon the willows'. Some have wedded themselves to new pursuits, and appear in another character as historians, novelists, or metaphysicians – poets no longer. Byron and Shelley have been snatched from us by untimely deaths; and Keats too, that bud of faintest promise, has suffered a too early blight. Let us lament the destiny which has thus closed their mortal and poetic career together, in the first summer of their lives, – but with a measured sorrow. [4]

This sense of loss was overwhelming. Victorian poets did not emulate the extraordinary ambitions of their Romantic precursors, with Shelley's, Wordsworth's and Keats's often fervid interests in states of consciousness that would overcome temporal conditions. The sublime – that exultant and ineffable feeling of joy which rises over and above the material world – bursts from the centre of Romantic aesthetics. This is not a central Victorian preoccupation, although it is possible to identify mid- and late nineteenth-century versions of the sublime, in modified and lessened form. Rather, it seems that young Victorians such as Tennyson and Browning absorbed, in their own distinctive ways, a sense of belatedness into their writing. In other words their work possesses a sense of coming after an event or movement they are unable to recover.

This question of belatedness is as much social and historical as specifically literary. To start writing and publishing in the 1830s was to be involved in a world very different from the one occupied by the Romantics whose political atmosphere was charged with the consequences of the French Revolution. Early Victorian Britain promised greater freedoms, and it is worth making some general points about these. Steps towards extending the franchise had been taken (1832); the Test and Corporation Acts debarring Dissenters from public service were now lifted (1828); the Roman Catholics had been emancipated (1829), as had slaves (1833); trades unions were gathering momentum; and the workers would have a powerful platform in the People's Charter (culminating in the late 1840s). Romantic writing developed during a perod that was altogether more oppressive, and so it is unsurprisingly infused with a rebellious energy that asserts the primacy of the self in a time of very harsh measures, such as the 'gagging acts', imposed in 1795 in response to the turmoil in France. The country was in the grip of Tory absolutist rule until Castlereagh's suicide in 1822. Early Victorian poetry reorientated itself to a society that was much more diverse, especially where class and gender were concerned. The workers, the middle classes and women of all classes were staking new claims on culture. Different societies ineluctably make different demands on the art of their age, and Browning's poetry is insistently Victorian in its idiom, form and, importantly, sense of post-Romantic disillusionment.

One poem may serve as a first example to bear out Browning's Victorian sense of being self-consciously post-Romantic. This is '"Transcendentalism: A Poem in Twelve Books"'. It is worth quoting all fifty-one lines of it, since the poem yields a number of major points about Browning's attitude to poetry, poets and their audiences.

> Stop playing, poet! May a brother speak?
> 'Tis you speak, that's your error. Song's our art:
> Whereas you please to speak these naked thoughts
> Instead of draping them in sights and sounds.
> – True thoughts, good thoughts, thoughts fit to treasure
>   up!   5
> But why such long prolusion and display,
> Such turning and adjustment of the harp,
> And taking it upon your breast, at length,
> Only to speak dry words across its strings?
> Stark-naked thought is in request enough: 10
> Speak prose and hollo it till Europe hears!
> The six-foot Swiss tube, braced about with bark,
> Which helps the hunter's voice from Alp to Alp –
> Exchange our harp for that, – who hinders you?

But here's your fault; grown men want thought, you think;   15
Thought's what they mean by verse, and seek in verse.
Boys seek for images and melody,
Men must have reason – so, you aim at men.
Quite otherwise! Objects throng our youth, 'tis true;
We see and hear and do not wonder much: 20
If you could tell us what they mean, indeed!
As German Boehme never cared for plants
Until it happed, a-walking in the fields,
He noticed all at once that plants could speak,
Nay, turned with loosened tongue to talk with him.   25
That day the daisy had an eye indeed –
Colloquized with cowslip on such themes!
We find them extant yet in Jacob's prose.
But by the time youth slips a stage or two
While reading prose in that tough book he wrote   30
(Collating and emendating the same
And settling on the sense most to our mind),
We shut the clasps and find life's summer past.
Then, who helps more, pray, to repair our loss –
Another Boehme with a tougher book   35
And subtler meanings of what roses say, –
Or some stout Mage like him of Halberstadt,
John, who made things Boehme wrote thoughts about?
He with a 'look you!' vents a brace of rhymes,
And in there breaks the sudden rose herself,   40
Over us, under, round us every side,
Nay, in and out the tables and the chairs
And musty volumes, Boehme's book and all, –
Buries us with a glory, young once more,
Pouring heaven into this shut house of life.   45

So come, the harp back to your heart again!
You are a poem, though your poem's naught.
The best of all you showed before, believe,
Was your own boy-face o'er the finer chords
Bent, following the cherub at the top   50
That points to God with his paired half-moon wings.

The general argument is quite straightforward, although some of the references may have struck Victorian readers as odd. The speaker reproves a younger poet for writing in a clumsily prosaic manner, failing to master the techniques of lyric poetry to elevate his wildly ambitious, and sadly leaden, philsophical subject matter (the 'transcendentalism' of the title). All great thinkers have had the urge to write of the natural wonders they have experienced. The Swedish mystic, Jacob Boehme, is offered as an example. But for Boehme's contact with nature to make poetic sense one needs to follow the example of someone like John of Halberstadt, an obscure medieval German priest, whose writings have the power to revive Boehme's heightened perceptions. Poetry, then, can recover things 'to repair our loss' (34). The trouble is, the young poet does not seem to understand that this is the case, and so he persists in writing in a dull and enervating style.

It goes without saying that '"Transcendentalism"' is a poem about poetry, and that poetry, when successful, is an art that 'Buries us with a glory' (44), makes us 'young once more' (44), and thereby brings 'heaven into this shut house of life' (45). The aim of poetry, then, is to usher God's beneficent power into the confines of this world to revitalise humanity. Yet these strongly religious words have resonances that go beyond the clear advice offered to a younger poet. Reading Browning here means turning to an earlier generation of poets to see how he is revising his own poetic inheritance. As with all artistic forms, poetry necessarily carries the burden of the past within it, if not always as consciously as here. '"Transcendentalism"' is notable because it concerns the importance of younger poets learning from older ones, and it performs this task by making a display of its generic heritage. Using a speaker who scorns the philosophical indulgences of a younger poet, Browning echoes, and transforms, a well known Romantic poem. That is to say, in using a speaker who is telling a younger poet how to write poetry properly, Browning in '"Transcendentalism"' is alluding to, and perhaps more importantly, *transfiguring*, one of his Romantic forebears. This is an ingenious textual manoeuvre, and it is by no means an unrepresentative example of Browning's powerfully ironising intelligence. The lines in question (44–5) are significant because they supply the guiding threads towards an intertextual matrix with Wordsworth's famous 'Ode: Intimations of Immortality from Recollections of Early Childhood', first published in 1807. [5]

The 'Ode' provides a pre-eminent example of one of Wordsworth's recurring themes: the question of how and why a child may exuberantly participate in the natural world, while an adult may not. As children, along with all things that thrive upon this earth, 'Give themselves up to jollity' (31), adults are left to contemplate their own sense of alienation from the joyous spectacle before them. Wordsworth notes that it is the fate of the adult mind to recognise that the grown up intellect is decisively separate from the jubilant spirit of childhood that seems at one with its surroundings. Counterpointing lyrical against meditative passages, the 'Ode' argues that the adult is placed in a paradoxical position regarding the child who is lovingly embraced by a generous, fecund and spiritually invigorating nature. Although the adult, having learned and refined skills in rational analysis, is able to comprehend the child's spontaneous pleasures, it is rationality itself that unfortunately estranges the adult from childhood bliss. Children do not reason; they just play.

But this does not stop Wordsworth from striving to recapture the energy of those first exhilarating moments. Even if 'there hath past away a glory from the earth' (18), Wordsworth's 'Ode' articulates a burning desire to overcome the disappointed ruminations of the mature 'philosophic mind' (190). The 'Ode', if keenly aware that 'nothing can bring back the hour / Of splendour in the grass' (181–2) beloved in childhood, manipulates its versatile Pindaric form to reanimate those early sensuous pleasures uniting humanity and nature in one, and so give a vibrant sense of that former 'visionary gleam' (56). Zestful innocence springs from its every line, as the following couplet, couched in the present tense, insists: 'The Rainbow comes and goes, / And lovely is the Rose' (10–11). The 'Ode' is inescapably caught in a tension between lilting forms of lyricism to represent childhood 'joy' while recognising, in its reflective moments, that such 'joy' can never be adequately expressed, since it is consigned to the past.

This typically Romantic conundrum – acknowledging that innocence is lost while using poetry in vain to recover it – lies at the heart of Browning's '"Transcendentalism"'. Both Wordsworth's and Browning's respective poems are closely connected in terms of content and vocabulary. In particular, one word and its derivatives that turns up repeatedly in the 'Ode' is important here, and this is 'glory' (16, 18, 57, 64, 83, 125, 182). In both the 'Ode' and '"Transcendentalism"', 'glory' signifies the auratic power of God's love in human life. In the 'Ode', 'glory' is the most strongly charged of several words which give the poem the explicit feeling of a prayer or invocation, as these lines indicate:

> Our birth is but a sleep and a forgetting:
> The Soul that rises with us, our life's Star,
>   Hath had elsewhere its setting,
>   And cometh from afar:
>   Not in entire forgetfulness,
>   And not in utter nakedness,
> But trailing clouds of glory do we come
>   From God, who is our home:
> Heaven lies about us in our infancy!
> Shades of the prison-house begin to close
>   Upon the growing Boy
> But he beholds the light, and whence it flows,
>   He sees it is his joy.
>   (58–70)

Like an incandescent shooting star, 'glory' is synonymous with the visible flame of God, irradiating through all living elements within the universe. Children have the closest attachment to this burning energy and so, in a sense, they embody divine love. As they grow up, God's light diminishes, since reason comes sadly to obscure it. The child, therefore, is the privileged communicant of divine knowledge and it is to children that adults must turn to comprehend the disconsolate fact that they, as grown ups, are dispossessed of theophanic wisdom.

Much of this would seem to pass into Browning's poem where the speaker claims that great poets unleash 'glory' (44) once they abandon mature 'reason' (18). A boyish attitude towards 'images and melody' (17) is more likely by far to produce excellent poetry. Likewise, once this 'glory' has covered the earth, the poet's splendid rhymes will proliferate like roses: Browning's 'sudden rose' (40) has been grafted onto Wordsworth's 'Lovely Rose' (21). There are several other echoes. In his 'shut house of life' (45), Browning revises Wordsworth's gloomy 'prison-house' (67). More generally, Wordsworth's pastoral 'sweet May-morning' (44), where children are 'culling /On every side/In a thousand valleys far and wide,/Fresh flowers' (45–8), is reimagined by Browning in Boehme's encounter with nature – a moment of astonishing revelation to the mystic who discovered that the daisy and the cowslip could 'talk' (25). There are, then, remarkable convergences between these two poems.

Yet the points of difference between them are equally, if not more, pronounced. Whereas Wordsworth's speaker takes the position of one who speaks directly to an audience (there is a narrator whose speech opens with the declarative 'There was a time . . .' (1)), Browning's has a specific form of address: 'Stop playing, poet!' (1). In '"Transcendentalism"' there would seem to be an implied auditor or addressee, and so the reader may be thought to overhear or witness one part of a colloquy between two poets. As far as genre is concerned these poems take antithetical forms, Wordsworth's ode deploying rhyme, Browning's using blank verse. And where the ode makes for a limber movement between clauses, Browning's syntax operates by fits and starts. Wordsworth speaks of nebulous things: 'Fallings from us, vanishings' (147), and 'shadowy recollections' (153); while Browning's vocabulary, by contrast, tends towards quick movements and snap decisions: here 'youth slips a stage or two' (29) (it does not fade); he 'shuts the clasps' (33) of Boehme's book; and John of Halberstadt, via a mixed metaphor, 'vents a brace of rhymes' (39). There is an indecorous abruptness, an unsettling impatience, a muscular energy, in Browning's poem. Finally, Wordsworth's poem has a conventional title, while Browning's, placed in quotation marks, mocks the pretensions of the young poet's epic.

These observations lead to one further point. Where Wordsworth's 'Ode' moves stage by stage to explore the problem of the adult's estrangement from childhood joy, '"Transcendentalism"' adopts an altogether more assured, even arrogant, stance. The young poet is addressed by an imperative as the speaker makes plain statements about the virtues and – more emphatically – vices of poetry. Browning's older poet easily finds fault. Juxtaposed to the 'Ode', Browning's poem seems to be performing a surprising function. By abstracting the general argument of the 'Ode', and so vouching for boyish spontaneity, the speaker of '"Transcendentalism"' sounds more like a disinterested critic remarking on poetry. All too conspicuously, he does not practise what he preaches. In his forceful tone of voice, this older poet is in full command of poetic authority. He claims to know what is best. But he fails to comply with his prescriptions. Demanding sweet lyricism from the younger poet, he delivers a hard-headed, and precisely reasoned, argument. Encouraging the younger poet to go back to his harp, he himself plays an altogether different tune. It is as if the kind of poetry the speaker would like to hear can be produced neither by the younger poet nor, indeed, himself. The desired lyricism is absent. The ideal poem that should be written has failed to emerge. Instead there is the 'prose Browning' that Wilde deemed to be the mark of the poet's originality. Why is '"Transcendentalism"' so paradoxically structured in this way?

In its conceptual peculiarity – where form and theme seem to be at odds – '"Transcendentalism"' is by no means unusual in Browning's canon. Jolting, quirky, more critical than lyrical, this poem points towards poetry without, somehow, becoming the poem it would appear to approve of. It could be said that '"Transcendentalism"' is the spectre of a poem, giving voice to a poet who would appear not to be composing poetry while simultaneously proffering advice on the form and function of the genre. The speaker, we might imagine, is supposed to be in conversation, and Browning has trapped him, perhaps off guard, into a poem which can be attributed to nobody in particular. But these are puzzling speculations. Who, indeed, does the title '"Transcendentalism"' belong to? Who is the author of it? Browning, the speaker, or the younger poet? Raising questions such as these makes Browning especially confounding, and interesting. Having learned some vital lessons from Wordsworth, Browning's experienced and knowledgeable poet – who sounds like a critic – occupies a somewhat eccentric place here: outside the poetic tradition in which Browning would have appeared to have situated him. By treating the poetic voice in this way Browning had created an entirely new space in which poetry could operate. This may be called for convenience a metapoetic space: a kind of critical commentary taking place on the margins of poetic tradition but still within poetry itself.

'Popularity', also from *Men and Women*, adopts a similar stance, but this time Browning uses the idea of the metapoem to outline a more complex theory of poetic creativity. The point of 'Popularity' is to make distinctions between true and false artists, and it suggests why second rate writers achieve fame at the expense of their superiors. Like '"Transcendentalism"',

'Popularity' in part takes its bearings from a Romantic precursor, on this occasion Keats, whose outrageous treatment by the periodical press in the 1810s was forcefully brought to the attention of the early Victorians with Richard Monckton Milnes's edition of the *Life and Letters* in 1839. Browning's closing question is 'What porridge had John Keats?' (65). He is wondering what justice there was for a young poet whose early death almost threw his work into complete obscurity. Browning's intricate poem, which makes very rapid moves between idea and image, counts as one of the most difficult (and, in fact, least read) in his collection of 1855. Yet it is the one which perhaps throws most light on Browning's post-Romantic anxiety – which is that popularity may elude even those poets who bring the shining gift of God's 'glory' into this world. Poets of the highest genius may pass either misunderstood or, worse, unnoticed. This was very nearly the fate of Keats. Moreover, 'Popularity' was the poem that John Ruskin chose to comment on at length in a detailed letter to Browning shortly after *Men and Women* had been published. Ruskin's letter provides the most exhaustive critique undertaken by any of Browning's literary peers. Placed together, the poem, the poetic theory it espouses, and Ruskin's somewhat bemused response, indicate a great deal about why Browning's poetry struck many of its readers as elliptical, if not downright perplexing.

The first three stanzas introduce a painter who wants to depict a poet; once more, a harsh imperative serves to grab the attention of an implied auditor:

Stand still, true poet that you are!
　I know you; let me try and draw you.
Some night you'll fail us: when afar
　You rise, remember one man saw you,
Knew you, and named a star!

My star, God's glow-worm! Why extend

That loving hand of his which leads you,
Yet locks you safe from end to end
    Of this dark world, unless he needs you,
Just saves your light to spend?

His clenched hand shall unclose at last,
    I know, and let out all the beauty:
My poet holds the future fast,
    Accepts the coming ages' duty, –
Their present for this past.

(1–15)

These rather compacted lines sort out an intricate network of
relationships between the painter, the poet and God – each of
whom has a different but connected function. God, as might be
expected, invests the poet with inspirational light, and it is up
to the Deity to choose when to 'unclose' this divine glory and
set its 'beauty' free into the world. The poet, then, is a kind of
receptacle or medium for divine knowledge or prophecy – the
poet is able to imagine the future in the present age. He is, in
other words, the *vates* or seer lauded since classical times, and
upheld as a hero in the Victorian period by Thomas Carlyle,
whom Browning admired.[6] He is also, implicitly, the visionary
of the Romantic period. Yet from the way the painter speaks, it
might appear that the poet is unaware of this fact. The painter
asserts that he knows the truth of this matter, and that it is up
to him to point this out to the poet. By painting him, this artist
can give a true picture of the poet; and so, in later lines, he
decides to portray his subject as a Greek fisherman, drawing in
nets full of murex, the crustacean that yields the iridescent
purple dye used, in fact, in painting.

Already, it should be clear that 'Popularity' is not only a
poem concerned with the creation of poetry; it is also interested
in structures of representation – whereby a painter pictures a
poet in a scene where the materials that make the painter's art

are being landed in nets. There are, in all, three concepts or scenes of creativity at stake here. First, God's creation of the poet; second, the painter's depiction of the poet; and third, the poet's symbolic action of bringing a beautiful dye into the world – which enables the painter to picture him. Just as God creates poets, poets create great art, which in turn gives others, such as this painter, the opportunity to acknowledge that this is the case. Browning's poem, therefore, is trying to explain how one kind of art can account for the divine properties of another. Art, by inference, needs art to represent its divine purpose in this world. 'Popularity' suggests that only artists can discriminate between geniuses and their imitators. Although derivative painters such as 'Hobbs, Nobbs, Stokes and Nokes combine/ To paint the future from the past' (58–9) by putting tyrian 'blue into their line' (60), and so win favour with the public, it remains the duty of the painter who knows the meaning of art to give credit where it is due and thus praise the 'true poet' (1) for what he is worth. The commercial success of Hobbs and Nobbs rides on the back of the real genius, like Keats, who brought the original 'ocean-plunder . . . to land' (24–5).

Ruskin was at times thrown off course by the poem, although he clearly understood and admired parts of it, and obviously he thought it sufficiently important to write an extensive set of notes raising numerous queries. Examining the opening lines, he asked Browning:

> (Does this mean: literally – stand still? or where was the poet figuratively going – and why couldn't he be drawn as he went?) Some night you'll fail us? (Why some *night*? – rather than some day? – 'Fail us'. Now? Die?) When afar you Rise – (Where? – Now?) remember &c. (very good – I understand.[)] My star, God's glowworm. (Very fine. I understand and like that.)[7]

Phrase by phrase, Ruskin compiled an exacting inventory of those phrases he comprehended, and those (the majority) that

baffled him. He elicited this generous but firmly defensive reply
from Browning:

> For the hopes you entertain of what may become of subsequent
> readings, – all success to them! For your bewilderment more
> especially noted – how shall I help *that*? We don't read poetry by
> the same law; it is too clear. I cannot begin writing poetry by the
> same law; it is too clear. I cannot begin writing poetry till my
> imaginary reader had conceded licenses to me which you demur
> altogether. I *know* that I don't make out my conception by
> language, all poetry being a putting the infinite within the finite.
> You would have me paint it all plain out, which can't be; but by
> various artifices I try to make shift with touches and bits of outlines
> which *succeed* if they bear the conception from me to you.[8]

Here, in one of clearest explications he ever made of his art,
Browning states that his poetry by definition cannot be rendered 'plain'. Instead, he requires some concessions on the
reader's part, as if the poem would remain an unfinished
product without some kind of external assistance. This is the
assumption on which Browning bases much of his poetry: he
anticipates the reader broaching the gaps in meaning that are
inevitably left open. For Browning obviously sees poetry as a
somewhat incapacitated device. He says that it involves
'putting the infinite within the finite', itself an impossible act.
Poetry, it appears, is a fragile vehicle for the divine gift it has to
bear. Although true poetry may bury us 'with a glory', it can
only do so when readers allow it to. It is not complete in itself.
So it follows that the young poet of 'Popularity' needs the
painter's skill to bring his genius into view. Artists, Browning
says, need sympathetic audiences, no matter how small ('few or
none to watch and wonder' (22)).

This was a position he had held for many years. In his preface
to *Paracelsus*, his second major work, he called on the
interaction of the reader's 'co-operating fancy' to connect 'the

scattered lights into one constellation',[9] and this demand is built into many of his poems – sometimes explicitly, as in *Sordello*, and less conspicuously in the monologues, poems which subtly and gradually alert their readers that these dramas in miniature require active interpretation. In the poem that confirmed his place in the pantheon, *The Ring and the Book*, Browning directly addressed his readers twice as follows: 'British Public, ye who like me not' (I. 410, 1379). The first book of the poem not only lays out a groundplan explaining the general design of the plot it is setting out, but also attempts to persuade his readers ('you London folk' (I.422)) that they are an integral part of the work. Without them, it could not make sense – or, more correctly, be made to make sense. Browning's poetry devises structures which anticipate a dialogue with its readership. If these poems are frequently about the creation of poetry, they are, then, also deeply concerned with the way they are being – or should be – read.

Browning knew that he was making novel demands on his readers, just as he was thoroughly aware that his approach to poetry was markedly different from that of his Romantic forefathers. Wordsworth, Keats and Shelley did not thematise the production, function and consumption of poetry in their work to the degree that Browning did since their work was part of a movement which it was left to a younger group of writers, such as Browning, to explicate. One further document, his best known account of poetry, strengthens and extends some of the main issues raised so far and provides an introduction to the concerns of the dramatic monologue, which is the focus of all the ensuing chapters. In 1852 Browning published his long 'Introductory Essay' to a collection of letters reputed to be by Shelley (they turned out to be forgeries). This article is commonly known as the 'Essay on Shelley'. In it Browning discusses two related types of poet, whom he calls for convenience the 'subjective' and the 'objective'. These rather loose terms had been in circulation in Britain from the 1830s, and periodical reviewers made somewhat inconsistent use of them. By 'subjective', Browning is thinking of the type of poet who is intimately bound to God; this poet's eye turns to 'Not what man sees, but what God sees – the *Ideas* of Plato, seeds of creation lying burningly on the Divine Hand – it is toward these that he struggles.' A poet of mind, he is a 'seer' (*vates*), rather than a 'fashioner' (*poietes*).[10] By contrast, the 'objective' poet is more involved with the world around him. He works in close conjunction with his audience (p. 1001):

> The auditory of such a poet will include, not only the intelligences which, save for such assistance, would have missed the deeper meaning and enjoyment of the original objects, but also the spirits of a like endowment with his own, who, by means of his abstract, can forthwith pass to the reality it was made from, and either corroborate their impressions of things known already, or supply themselves with new from whatever shows in the inexhaustible variety of existence may have hitherto escaped their knowledge.

Browning does not place these poetic types in a hierarchy: 'It would be idle to inquire, of these two kinds of poetic faculty in operation, which is the higher or even rarer endowment' (p. 1003). Instead, they represent tendencies along a scale connecting humanity and divinity. (Although Browning nowhere makes the suggestion, it is often inferred that he identifies himself with the 'objective' poet whose 'endeavour has been to reproduce things external' (p. 1001), and whose work is predominantly 'dramatic', appealing to the 'aggregate human mind' (p. 1003).) The prominence of each type is said to vary from one age to another, according to the dictates of Providence. At times there will be a decisive break in the kind of poetry needed by a culture, and this involves the radical reworking of poetic tradition: 'getting at substance by breaking the assumed wholes into parts of independent and unclassed value, careless of the unknown laws for re-combining them (it will be the business of yet another poet to suggest those hereafter)' (p. 1004). These remarks, especially the closing parenthesis, are significant because they show Browning's definite awareness of how a younger generation of poets redefines the laws of those who have gone before them, thereby 'Shaping for their uses a new and different creation from the last' (p. 1004). Age by age, one generation displaces the achievements of another 'by a right of life over death' (p. 1004), rising by degrees upon the slopes of Parnassus. In sum, he saw it was his role to make poetry anew.

By taking '"Transcendentalism"' and 'Popularity' together it is reasonable to claim that Browning apprehends that it is his own 'business' to reveal 'the unknown laws' which bring innovative poetry, trailing clouds of glory, into the world. This is most certainly the case with the way he treats Shelley, whose poetry he knew perhaps more thoroughly, and admired more greatly, than any of the Romantics. The extent of Shelley's influence on Browning has been the subject of extensive discussion, notably in Harold Bloom's criticism, with its Freudian emphasis on the Oedipal struggles that young poets undergo in the face of their elders' artistic power. In such cases, the 'sons' initiated into the poetic tradition develop highly resistant reaction formations against the influence of their 'fathers'.[11] And there is the temptation to see Browning's work as an extended argument working through and against both the discoveries and errors of Shelley. Browning's first published poem, *Pauline*, adopts Shelley's style in praise of him. Like so many of Browning's poems, it is a self-conscious work, fully aware of what it means to imitate an idol. Browning certainly believed it was his vocation to itemise the divine laws governing Shelley's writing, seeing in the master's politically and sexually controversial career a gathering movement towards the recognition of the divine wisdom that Shelley, as an atheist, so eagerly denounced. Browning reads Shelley's Platonic idealism as testimony to the deeply religious, and implicitly Christian, knowledge contained in the poet's works (pp. 1009–10):

25

Gradually he was raised above the contemplation of spots and the attempt at effacing them, to the great Abstract Light, and, through the discrepancy of the creation, to the sufficiency of the first Cause. Gradually he was learning that the best way of removing abuses is to stand fast by truth. Truth is one, as they are manifold; and innumerable negative effects are produced by the upholding of one positive principle. I shall say what I think, – had Shelley lived he would have finally ranged himself with the Christians; his very instinct for helping the weaker side (if numbers make strength), his very 'hate of hate', which at first mistranslated itself into delirious Queen Mab notes and the like, would have got clearer-sighted by exercise.

This is an arresting argument. It is extraordinary to claim that Shelley was a Christian without realising it – as though the poet's atheism were simply an immature aberration, rather than a wholehearted challenge to the moral order. Only the follies of his youth, it would appear, had understandably led Shelley away from the Christian God to whom his mature self would have been reconciled. Once a proper biography of the poet has been written, Browning declares, then 'the most doubtful' aspects of Shelley's reputation 'will be found consistent with a belief in the eventual perfection of his character, according to the poor limits of our humanity' (p. 1007). Browning's authoritative posturing here may seem to verge on the magnanimous, vaunting that he knows more about Shelley's art than Shelley knew himself. But the point he is making is a historical one: Browning, from his post-Romantic position, claims he has the gift of hindsight to forgive Shelley's many personal and religious failings. It is as if by virtue of being so endowed with God's prophetic gift that Shelley remained blind to it. Failure, in any case, is for Browning a fundamental human quality. Even poets as remarkably endowed with God's love as Shelley have to live within 'the poor limits of our humanity': 'An absolute vision is not for this world, but we are permitted a continual approximation to it' (p. 1005). In spite of himself, Browning states, Shelley was growing closer and closer to the God he had spurned.

If Browning clearly apprehends why Shelley failed to understand the divine love infused in poetry, it should not amaze us to find that Browning never aspires towards God in a confident and positive manner. Robbed of the 'absolute vision' sought by Romantic visionaries, Browning's poetry turns its attentions to the human limitations, the finite boundaries, in which it is obliged to make God's love known. His profound sense of limitation is manifest in both the form and content of his poems. A glance at his multifarious cast of characters reveals all sorts of strange, debased and far from perfect men and women. He frequently trades in liars, tricksters, casuists, and criminal types who would seem to have fallen – or are on the verge of falling – from grace. Such people often slyly manipulate language to their own ends, striving to conceal the truth of their despicable actions from those who hear their rambling speeches. And their rhetorical gestures and syntactical manoeuvres are correspondingly peculiar.

Although Browning does not write in a uniform style there is a characteristically compressed grammar that prevails in his work, and which gives his poetry its own distinctive stamp. His personae, whether they are attempting to deceive their audiences or not, tend to speak in halting phrases broken up with awkward exclamations and intrusive questionings. They routinely elide verbs, yoking ideas together in unexpected forms of apposition. Sentences can run on unendingly for line after line until the main clause is buried under a pile of verbal debris, and the logical sense of the sentence vanishes. The style is atomistic. Parentheses turn into extended digressions, as if the poem were resisting linear movement. Similarly, the vocabulary can be strikingly bizarre. Archaisms regularly crop up; neologisms abound; compound forms burgeon. Moreover, there are rhythmical lurches in units where prominent stresses are extraordinarily high in number for English poetry. Finally, there is the sound of it all. So jerkily consonantal is Browning's writing that Gerard Manley Hopkins remarked that reading Browning was like listening to an intemperate man jumping up and down and shouting with his mouth full of bread and cheese.[12]

The opening lines of *The Ring and the Book* bear out some of these points:

> Do you see this Ring?
>   'T is Rome-work, made to match
> (By Castellani's imitative craft)
> Etrurian circlets found, some happy morn,
> After a dropping April; found alive
> Spark-like 'mid unearthed slope-side figtree-roots
> That roof old tombs at Chiusi: soft, you see,
> Yet crisp as jewel-cutting. There's one trick,
> (Craftsmen instruct me) one approved device
> And but one, fits such slivers of pure gold
> As this was, – such mere oozings from the mine,
> Virgin as oval tawny pendent tear
> At beehive-edge when ripened combs o'erflow, –
> To bear the file's tooth and the hammer's tap:
> Since hammer needs must widen out the round,
> And file emboss it fine with lily-flowers,
> Ere the stuff grow a ring-thing right to wear.
>   (I. 1–17)

Inviting the reader to examine the symbolic design of the ring, the narrator instantly begins to fashion this piece of gold into 'a figure, a symbol, say' (I. 31) of the poem he is creating. Beaten, flattened, elaborated, the ring provides the guiding metaphor for the whole shape of this epic. It would seem to bring all the disparate parts of the narrative into one fully rounded shape – although there has been some dispute as to the exact meaning of this highly suggestive metaphor. The same goes for the syntax. Glancing asides; inserted parentheses; appended figures: all these features draw together discrete elements (provenance of the gold; its geographical location; and its luxuriant texture). Noticeably, the two intervolved sentences run back on themselves, looping key words together – 'there's *one* trick . . . *one* approved device/And but *one*'; '*such* slivers . . . *such* mere oozings'. These adjectives stress both individuation and connectedness: the trick is also a device which makes the gold suitably manipulable to the craftsman's file; the slivers are also oozings which are in the process of being transformed into a 'ring-thing'. Certainly, the gold, like the syntax, is not static matter; it is 'soft' and 'crisp' at once.

Constantly remaking themselves, these sentences bear out Tucker's chief insight that Browning's 'is an art of disclosure, an art that resists of its own finalities'.[13] That is, the poem keeps matter in motion. As the malleable syntax reveals, Browning's writing is structured on a principle of deferral or delay, as if it were attempting to make each and every textual element equally present; hence the tendency to divagate, rather than place things in sequential order. This tactic enables Browning to keep the analogies he is drawing up between the craftsman's art and his own in a buoyant state of play. Just as Castellani exercises his 'imitative craft', so too does the poem attempt to imitate the creation of the ring. Similarly, where the craftsman deploys his skills to remodel the ring on 'Etrurian circlets', Browning's poem applies itself to reviving the historical past. *The Ring and the Book*, therefore, is all too clearly aware of its 'imitative' status, and the craft that gives poetry its shape.

Browning's desire to make analogies between one art form and his own prompted some of the most brilliant Victorian parodies. The best of these, by C. S. Calverley, wittily exaggerates the slips and breaks characterising Browning's condensed grammar. Here is the opening of 'The Cock and the Bull':

You see this pebble-stone? It's a thing I bought
Of a bit of a chit of boy i' the mid o' the day –
I like to dock the smaller parts-o'-speech,
As we curtail the already cur-tail'd cur
(You catch the paronomasia, play 'po' words?)
Did, rather, i' the pre-Landseerian days.
Well, to my muttons. I purchased the concern,
And clapt it i' my poke, having given for same
By way o' chop, swop, barter or exchange –
'Chop' was my snickering dandiprat's own term –
One shilling and fourpence, current coin o' the realm.[14]

Calverley, with punishing wit, makes Browning into a painfully overclever stylist whose strange idiom is not only extremely mannered but also rather vulgar. It is the language of the lower middle classes: those who prize semi-precious stones washed up on the beach, rather than gold. These are people obsessed with shillings and pence. They lack culture.

Although this parody necessarily distorts its subject, it does highlight Browning's distinctly bourgeois perception of the market – which is where the opening of *The Ring and the Book* is set. Browning is eager to inform his readership of the techniques which give the ring (and, by analogy, the poem) its material as well as artistic value. 'Imitative craft' has to be understood for what it is – the work of someone who has struggled hard to fashion his wares, and Browning, as a worthy middle-class individual, is toiling hard at his God-given labour. His language seeks to enact that sense of a participative, perhaps market-bound, process: it, like the ring, is something in exchange with its audience, and, between them, poet and audience have to work out the value of the 'ring' and the 'book' – and how each acts as a metaphor for the other. (*The Ring and the Book* entwines around a double figure. Browning's 'book' – his poem – is imaged as a circumambient 'ring'; his source – the Old Yellow Book – is valued as highly as a piece of gold jewellery.)

On occasions this strenuously awkward style has been labelled 'grotesque'. Walter Bagehot's Victorian adoption of this adjective in 1864, possibly after Ruskin's discussion of the 'grotesque' art of the Renaissance in *Modern Painters III* (1856), is uncomplimentary. Bagehot joins with a tradition of hostile critics who, like George Santayana, see Browning's writing as a 'poetry of barbarism', as careless and half formed in thought and structure.[15] Alfred Austin, in one of his polemical articles on 'The Poetry of the Period', argued in 1869 that 'Browning is muddy and musical to the last degree . . . He has no voice, and yet he wants to sing. He is not a poet, and yet he would fain write poetry.'[16] There is some truth in these demeaning remarks, although Austin remains unaware of the deliberate lengths to which Browning went to accomplish this obscure style. For Browning could write very lyrically indeed – 'Home Thoughts from Abroad' (1845) certainly counts among his best known and most mellifluous poems. Yet the 'grotesque' predominates.

Exploring Bagehot's claims, Isobel Armstrong observes Browning's 'insistent, almost wilful, delight in inchoateness', and adds that this 'springs from a belief that experience cannot be structured and a scepticism about the capacity of language to express the true structure of our experience'.[17] Language, above all, is an unwieldly instrument, scattering rather than consolidating meaning. In *Sordello*, which employs his most anfractuous syntactical and grammatical forms, Browning refers to this style as 'Communication different' (VI. 600). It was a wholly intentional act – one that flouted poetic convention to create an uncompromisingly individualised poetry. As his famous letter to Ruskin demonstrates, Browning would never stray from his principles. This left him, as the member of a new (because belated) generation of poets, in an unusual situation where he was exceptionally confident about the deficiencies of the linguistic forms he used. He took many opportunities to explain this negativity, and it made him into an energetically

sceptical writer – one far removed from the naive conversation-
alist depicted in rather patronising terms by Benson.

Reading Browning, therefore, is to engage with a poet whose
work foregrounds its post-Romantic consciousness – that has
internalised, and made complex, what it means to read and be
read. Bloom emphasises this point:

> Of all the problematic elements in Browning's poetry, what
> increasingly seems the central challenge is the peculiar nature of
> Browning's rhetorical stance. No poet has evidenced more than
> Browning so intense a will-to-power over the interpretation of his
> own poems. The reader rides through the Browning country with
> the poet always bouncing along at his side overinterpreting
> everything.[18]

This 'overinterpretative' impulse is particularly noticeable in
the dramatic monologue, a poetic form which knows in
advance how it should be interpreted. Whatever surprises the
monologue may spring upon its readers, there is the uncanny
sense that Browning has contrived it, and enjoyed it, before
anybody else. Yet this sense of having beaten us to the post
appears to leave him with a great sense of unease. As he notes
in *The Ring in the Book*, 'ye who like me not . . . will have your
proper laugh/At the dark question' – by which he means the
morally confounding plot set before us. 'Laugh it!' he com-
mands, and then asserts: 'I laugh first' (I. 410–12). But it is a
discomforting laughter. To have read his poem before anyone
else is both Browning's privilege and his problem. And it is to
the anticipatory energies of his dramatic poetry that the next
chapter turns.

2

Dramatising Lyric

Writing in 1856, George Eliot was among a small minority who understood the intellectual demands made by Men and Women:

> To read poems is often a substitute for thought: fine-sounding conventional phrases and the sing-song of verse demand no co-operation in the reader; they glide over his mind with the agreeable unmeaningness of 'the compliments of the season', or a speaker's exordium of 'feelings too deep for expression'. But let him expect no drowsy passivity in reading Browning. Here he will find no conventionality, no melodious commonplace, but freshness, originality, sometimes eccentricity of expression; no didactic laying-out of a subject, but dramatic indication, which requires the reader to trace by his own mental activity the underground stream of thought that jets out in elliptical and pithy verse. To read Browning he must exert himself, but he will exert himself to some purpose. [1]

Appearing in the *Westminster Review*, where Eliot worked as a junior editor, this counted among the very best reviews Browning received in what was a rather mixed batch. The

Westminster, established in 1824 as a rostrum for Utilitarian ideas, was still by mid-century noted for its progressive liberal principles, and it provided the most rigorous political alternative to the prevailing Toryism of the major periodicals. The politics of the *Westminster* was significant for Browning because he, in many ways, was party to it. Although he did not move among the literary circles close to Eliot (who belonged, in any case, to a younger generation of radical thinkers), and although he was never noted for political activism of any kind, his attachments were to overlapping sets of London Utilitarians (followers of Jeremy Bentham) and Unitarians (disciples of Joseph Priestley) who had between them created something of a counter-culture that drew on liberal beliefs which were republican in spirit and egalitarian by nature. Such people brought about considerable shifts in Victorian thought, particularly in relation to concepts of liberty and justice. This was not so much a politics of class as a politics of the individual, one that gathered its strength during a time of considerable social unrest. Committed to individual freedoms, the Utilitarians and the liberals who followed in their wake penetrated deeper and deeper into the complexities of the individual mind: one of their main achievements was the psychological investigation of specific mental states.

Beginning with James Mill's exploration of mental 'associationism' in the 1820s, these radicals paved the way for Herbert Spencer's *Principles of Psychology* (1855), to which Eliot's fiction is, in many respects, indebted. Eliot was writing out of a context particularly responsive to the vibrant 'mental activity' conspicuously at work in Browning's dramatic poetry. She sees his '"majestic obscurity" . . . avowedly appealing to the mind of his reader', and fully appreciates how and why 'he sets our thoughts at work rather than our emotions'. Soliciting the reader's active interpretation of his dramatic poems, Browning produces art that 'pierces into all the secrets of human character'.[2] Few apart from Eliot were in a position to grasp the reasons for the interest in mind motivating these uncompromising poems.

By the time *Men and Women* was published, Browning had been experimenting with dramatic poetry for over twenty years, and his skills with the monologue were fully developed. In 1835 he saw fit to declare in his Preface to *Paracelsus*: 'I do not very well understand what is called a Dramatic Poem.'[3] Extracts from his correspondence of this period also indicate that his thoughts on the matter were somewhat inchoate. Writing to his close friend Amédée de Ripert-Monclar (a Bourbon from whom Browning may have been attempting to gain patronage), he identifies and then extrapolates his thoughts on two types of dramatic writing: the closet drama and the monologue, both of which he was composing with equal enthusiasm at this time. Dramatic poetry, he claims, is a kind of writing whose full significance is still forming in his mind:

The conditions of the *Drama* are well known: – those of what is popularly termed the *Poem* no less so: I cannot but conceive that, inasmuch as the canons of either have a reference to the peculiar ordering & exposition of each, the particular advantages offered by each, are *really* advantages only as long as its original purpose is kept in view, & that, for the most part, all attempts retain *one* without letting go the *other* – are signal failures, whether they be on the one hand, what are good-naturedly styled '*Poetical Plays*' – wherein the characters are possessed by a self consciousness truly exemplary which prompts them to develop their own constitution of head and heart systematically on every occasion with the utmost perspicuity & minuteness of detail, with every assistance from mood and figure: or on the other, those anomalous productions called '*Dramatic Poems*' wherein all the restrictions submitted to for their sake of compensating advantages in the original scheme (which regarded public representation) are scrupulously retained for some undiscovered fitness in themselves, & all the new facilities which the method they pursue places at their disposal, as pertinaciously rejected . . . Now, select any Drama you please, which comprises the history of a Thought or a Passion, &, putting

35

yourself in the position of author, view it as a conception of your own & consider that, having rêvé [dreamed] this History, you are about to give it a permanent existence . . . to reduce it to language. Do you desire it shall be *Read* not *Acted*? Follow throughout the whole, only what Raleigh calls the '*mind* of the piece', as a purple thread through the varied woof . . . discarding as unnecessary, the external machinery which would develop it, & only preserving the *Result* which was to be traced, however dimly through – then expand this *simple mood* – & you will have a Poem like my own [i.e. *Paracelsus*].[4]

Tentatively, and rather elliptically, Browning reveals that he is attempting to forge a hybrid kind of writing which meshes particular features from poetry and drama. What interests him is that both the 'poetical play' and the 'dramatic poem' can serve as vehicles for developing psychological characteristics which are in some way 'exemplary' – as if they might be teaching a lesson. By shifting drama from the stage on to the page, whereby the persona has to account for its own 'constitution of heart and head' as the poem unfolds, Browning is devising a poetry that emphasises the '"*mind* of the piece"'. For him, dramatic poetry can give greater permanency to – and, likewise, provide a history for – thoughts and moods that, in stage drama, cannot be interpreted with such intensity. Reducing moods and thoughts to 'language', and so removing them from the arena of acting, Browning aims to make the mind *readable*.

The impulse to create dramatic poetry was doubtless spurred by Browning's close involvement with the group of radicals associated with the controversial Unitarian preacher, W. J. Fox, who edited the remarkable *Monthly Repository* from 1827 to 1835, and wrote extensively on poetry in the 1820s and 1830s from a Utilitarian point of view. Although Browning had contacts in various sectors of literary society (he was connected with a theatrical circle, including William Charles Macready,

John Forster and Charles Dickens), his links with Fox created the conditions for his distinctive aesthetic choices. Fox, whom Browning variously described as his 'old praiser',[5] as well as his 'Chiron in a small way',[6] was a formative influence on the poet from an early age. He had advised Browning on some adolescent verses, which the precocious twelve-year-old duly consigned to the fire. Later, when Browning was in his early twenties, Fox treated him generously, introducing the aspiring poet to a group of established Dissenting intellectuals, which included Harriet Martineau and Thomas Noon Talfourd, and publishing some of the warmest reviews that *Pauline* and *Paracelsus* received. Under his, and then Leigh Hunt's, editorship, the *Repository* carried a handful of Browning's short poems.[7] The very first article printed in the *Westminster* was by Fox. His earliest reviews and essays demonstrate that he was part of a forward thinking middle-class intelligentsia searching for differrent cultural forms to assert an alternative politics based on Benthamite ideas.

It is probable that Browning, a voracious reader, knew Bentham's writings reasonably well, since he makes a joke about them in a letter to Ripert-Monclar.[8] Bentham's highly systematised Utilitarian philosophy argued that all moral and social acts should aim towards 'the greatest happiness to the greatest number': a motto which Bentham had abstracted from the writings of the Unitarian Priestley.[9] However, Bentham severely doubted the value of poetry, along with any imaginative arts. His objections are worth contemplating here, since Fox's essays, Browning's poetry, and importantly, the early prose of John Stuart Mill (the great liberal theorist) draw on and then modify Bentham's precepts to create an aesthetics concerned with qualities of mind. As Armstrong has written: 'Fox's aim was to deepen the Benthamite tradition by correcting misapprehensions of it and associating it above all with literature.'[10]

Bentham has frequently been subjected to exaggerated

claims that he was the ultimate enemy of poetry. Unswervingly logical in his approach to all areas of moral philosophy (from the making of laws to the building of prisons), Bentham condemned this art because he felt it was dangerously illogical. According to him, this unthinking form of representation gave pleasure to amuse and not improve its readership. It was an idiosyncratic view, one reached by taking eighteenth-century rationalism to extremes:

> Happiness depends upon the correctness of the facts with which our mind is furnished, and the rectitude of our judgement: but poetry has no very distinct tendency to produce either correctness of knowledge or rectitude of judgement. For one instance in which it has been employed to combat mischievous prejudices, a thousand might be cited in which they have been fostered and propagated by it. Homer is the greatest of poets: where shall we place him among moralists? Can any advantage be derived from the imitation of gods and heroes?[11]

Although this may seem a reductive account of poetry based on false dichotomies (proper pleasure is morally correct; poetry is mischievously prejudiced), it is complicated by the fact that Bentham developed an elaborate theory of fictions to describe the *representational* structure of the human world, particularly in relation to the operations of the law. By positing a theory of fictions, Bentham meant that the law was a potentially dangerous linguistic construction. He argued that language had to be ceaselessly disambiguated on all points of legislation. If law was a fiction for Bentham, it is not so surprising that he referred to poetry as a worryingly 'magic art' and builds up 'a superstructure of fictions'.[12]

Bentham carved out no space for a faculty of intuition which, to take a well known contemporary example, Coleridge realised in the concept of 'Imagination'. Beliefs in intuition were wholly alien to Bentham, and the opening sentences of his *Table of the Springs of Action* (1815) rail against doctrines of 'Ipsedixitism' – the groundrule (a conservative one) that states that human actions are governed by feelings. At times, Bentham referred to 'Ipsedixitism' as sentimentalism, where feelings may misguidedly govern thoughts. Instead, Bentham was concerned with the altogether rational motives determining human actions and the consequent pains and pleasures that they led to. He does, in fact, find a place for imagination in his exhaustive catalogue of 'springs of action'. But for him imagination cannot function as a form of transcendental inspiration, as it does in the writings of Coleridge and other major Romantics. Rather, Bentham sees imagination, not as an autonomous creative facility, but as a source of '*derivative* representations' of past perceptions that operates by placing its memory traces in a nonsequential order.[13] It should be clear, then, that Bentham's pursuit of social happiness placed the head above the heart. Contributors to the *Westminster* were at times in agreement with him: 'There are few great poets who have been good reasoners. They are the mere creatures of sentimental sympathy and antipathy; their heart tells them this, and their heart tells them that, their approbation and disapprobation, are measured by no intelligible standard.'[14]

Utilitarianism, however, held powerful attractions for middle-class activists such as Fox, whose politics was pledged to equality and, moreover, a *culture* that promoted egalitarianism. The Benthamites of Fox's circle were, in many ways, the heirs to the most radical voices of Romanticism, such as William Godwin and Shelley. In seeking to revise Bentham's aversion to imaginative writing, Fox contrived a new framework for understanding the 'mental states' present in poetry. Already, in 1830, he had offered this defence in the *Westminster*: 'The poet's sketch, as well as the painter's, should touch the heart, penetrating thither through the imagination as that does through the sight. A great master of the art can play upon the nervous system and produce and control its vibrations as easily as the well-practised performer can try the compass of a musical instrument.'[15] The most skilled artist, he argues, is in tune with the regulative laws of the 'nervous system'. In other words, he made much of the physical and material basis of poetry to justify its beneficial effects.

Similar analogies with anatomy, attempting to match bodily functions with psychological responses, are to be found in Fox's more sophisticated essay on *Poems, Chiefly Lyrical* by Alfred Tennyson. This review appeared in the *Westminster* in 1831. There, in Fox's striking formulation of poetic physiology, Tennyson 'seems to obtain entrance into a mind as he would make his way into a landscape: he climbs the pineal gland as if it were a hill in the centre of the scene'.[16] Yet Tennyson, Fox argues, is something far greater than an anatomist. He praises, above all, Tennyson's gift for 'impersonation', and views this outstanding quality as one that can and must be put to the best Utilitarian ends: poets 'can influence the associations of un-numbered minds . . . they can act with a force . . . upon national happiness'. It is, indeed, Tennyson's capacity to animate all sorts of states of mind that overwhelms Fox, although this ability to mine the passages of the mind troubles him slightly: 'Mr Tennyson has a dangerous quality in that facility of impersonation on which we have remarked, and by which he enters so thoroughly into the most strange and wayward idiosyncrasies of other men'.[17] Fox is no doubt thinking of Tennyson's finest monologues, such as 'Ulysses' and 'Tithonus', with which Browning must also have been acquainted; he seems to be hinting that Tennyson's faculty of 'impersonation' is so remarkable that it may render the integrity of each and every individual factitious. Perhaps it should not be a poet's duty to impersonate, and thus intrude upon, a person's mind?

Tennyson's dramatic poems, collected together with several ballads and many short lyrics in *Poems, Chiefly Lyrical*, lack the psychological intensity of the two monologues Browning would publish in the *Repository* in 1836. It is true to say that Tennyson's early works concentrate more on moods, passions and feelings. But when read alongside one another, those poems by Browning and Tennyson which give special prominence to the dramatic 'I' mark out a decisive shift towards a new poetry of mind. Before moving on to those early monologues by Browning, the changing shape of Utilitarian poetics needs to be traced in the figure of John Stuart Mill. For it is Mill who takes Fox's arguments a stage further by creating a theory of dramatic poetry which even more directly shares Browning's concerns.

Mill's two celebrated essays, 'What is Poetry?' and 'The Two Kinds of Poetry', appeared in the *Repository* in 1833, and they form part of his on-going concern with the nature of the imagination which Bentham had disregarded. Mill had been educated along strict Utilitarian lines; his father was, after Bentham, the most highly regarded philosopher in this field. In 1828, he suffered a mental breakdown. His *Autobiography* explains how and why he resorted 'to the internal culture of the individual' to recover his health. Although he 'never turned recreant to intellectual culture, or ceased to consider the power and practice of analysis as an essential condition both of individual and of social improvement', he found in Words-worth's poetry 'states of feeling . . . thought coloured by feeling, under the excitement of beauty'. [18] And this experience led him to theorise the precise workings of poetry on the mind and the body.

In the first of these two essays he is convinced that the 'object of poetry is confessedly to act upon the emotions'. [19] He shares Fox's concern with the poetry as an art which makes direct connections between internal mental 'associations' and their linguistic forms. Yet the conditions in which poetry finely attunes its language to reproduce the exact shapes of the feelings which underwrite it are different from other uses of rhetoric. He creates a distinction – one, as we shall see, some-what overturns itself – between dramatic and descriptive styles, favouring the latter. In fact, it would appear that by descriptive poetry he is thinking mostly of lyric. For it is the emotional immediacy of poetry that concerns him. This premise enables him to consider how in poetry one sees 'feeling confessing itself to itself, in moments of solitude, and bodying itself forth in symbols which are the nearest possible representations of the feeling in the exact shape in which it consists in the poet's mind' (p. 348). 'All poetry', he claims, 'is the nature of soliloquy' (p. 349). The poem, by this reckoning, is not involved in the social world; it is, instead, set apart, isolated, giving primacy to the internal conditions of the individual. He sums up its special nature in the following proposition: 'Eloquence is *heard*, poetry is *over*heard. Eloquence supposes an audience: the peculiarity of poetry appears in the poet's utter unconsciousness of a listener' (p. 348). Oratory is public; poetry is private. Drama addresses an audience; lyric speaks inwardly to the self.

Given Mill's implicit interest in lyric, and his fascination with self-reflexive outpourings of emotion, his essays of 1833 have on occasions been presented as examples of 'expressive' poetic theory. There is some truth in this. In his influential study of Romantic aesthetics, *The Mirror and the Lamp* (1953), M. H. Abrams observes Mill taking one of Wordsworth's main precepts to extremes. Wordsworth, in the first Preface to *Lyrical Ballads* (1800), claims that poetry should be 'the spontaneous overflow of powerful feelings'.[20] Mill concurred with this guiding principle to the degree that he gave a low priority to narrative elements in poetry. His interest in the sensuous properties of lyric makes him favour Shelley's poetry over the frequently meditative writings of Wordsworth (whose 'well', thought Mill, 'is never so full it overflows' (p. 358)). Staking the highest claims imaginable on the poet's unique temperament, Mill is led to controvert one of the determining concepts of poetry since classical times – that poetry is designed for an audience. According to Abrams, there is 'something singularly fatal to the audience' in Mill's point of view, and he adds that

Mill may have been led to this conclusion with the gradual disappearance of a unified reading public for poetry.[21]

That said, Mill's concern with '*overhearing*' suggests not so much an 'expressive' theory of poetry which altogether disregards its readership. Rather, it indicates that the audience is placed in an altogether different position from formerly, no longer directly addressed by the poet but indirectly listening in on the confession of feelings. Moreover, Mill certainly had an audience for poetry in his mind when he compared lyric to 'soliloquy', since the best poet, he argued, was like the finest actor: 'The actor knows that there is an audience present; but if he act as though he knew it, he acts ill' (p. 349). Lyric, therefore, has its place on a stage. It was up to Browning and, to a lesser extent, Tennyson to investigate the dramatic properties of the expressive lyric by putting its private utterances on public exhibition. By creating a structure whereby his speakers are '*overheard*', Browning opens up a space in which the authority of the poetic voice comes under scrutiny. For Browning's speakers make no claims on a general audience. They have altogether different reasons for breaking into speech. Their miniature dramas represent the peculiarities of their own individual characters. Sometimes soliloquising (unaware of a listener), sometimes addressing an implied auditor, they begin to say things that lack the sincerity, as well as universality, of their lyrical ancestors. Curious 'associations' and unaccountable intuitions occur in these strangely motivated poems, which take up issues of mental instability that the traditional lyric was not in a position to accommodate.

Mill's essays encouraged a wider examination of the dramatic dimensions to poetry. Several reviewers responded to Mill's essays by placing even more pressures on the staged element in poetry which was becoming more and more evident in the 1830s. A long historical poem, *Philip Van Artevelde* by Henry Taylor, was received with interest in 1834. The *Edinburgh* noted that it was a 'literary hybrid, combining in one both play and poem, without possessing the completeness, or fulfilling the purposes of either. Unlike the play, it cannot be represented on stage – unlike the poem, it excludes all description and sentiment, except such as may be conveniently placed in the mouth of some of the *dramatis personae*.' This writer argued, following Mill, that poetry 'should quicken and make clear our perception of the phenomena of thought and feeling – should teach us to trace the workings of our own minds, and comprehend more perfectly our relation to others'.[22] Dramatic poetry will tell us something about ourselves. But what exactly might those who '*overhear*' Browning's speakers discover about the complex workings of the mind?

'Johannes Agricola in Meditation', first published in 1836, presents an apologist for Antinomianism – a doctrine of predestination that avows that everybody shall be saved by God regardless of their actions on earth. Antinomian belief, with its commitment to predetermined ends, in part resembles Calvinist dogma. Given the context in which this poem first appeared, Antinomianism is certainly remote from the principles of Fox's Unitarianism, a faith which has no concern with concepts of salvation. Removed from Evangelical emphases on Original Sin, the atonement, and self-abnegation, Unitarians preserve a vision of human beings as innately good. Yet this is not a simply benevolent view of humanity. Since God's love dwells with each and every one of us, Unitarians argue that all people are capable of change through individual choices – to recognise and sustain the divine love inhabiting the soul. Our fates, in other words, have not been divinely preordained. Fox's readership, then, would have instantly seen that Johannes Agricola's faith was based on wholly mistaken assumptions. Confident that God shall spare his soul, Agricola reaches this extraordinary conclusion:

> I have God's warrant, could I blend
> All hideous sins, as in a cup,

To drink the mingled venoms up;
Secure my nature will convert
  The draught to blossoming gladness fast:
While sweet dews turn to the gourd's hurt,
  And bloat, and while they bloat it, blast,
  As from the first its lot was cast.
For as I lie, smiled on, full-fed
  By unexpected power to bless,
I gaze below on hell's fierce bed,
  And those its waves of flames oppress,
  Swarming in ghastly wretchedness;
Whose life on earth aspired to be
  One altar-smoke, so pure! – to win
If not love like God's love for me,
  At least to keep his anger in;
  And all their striving turned to sin.
Priest, doctor, hermit, monk grown white
  With prayer, the broken-hearted nun,
The martyr, the wan acolyte,
  The incense-swinging child, – undone
  Before God fashioned star or sun!
God, whom I praise; how could I praise,
  If such as I might understand,
Make out and reckon on his ways,
  And bargain for his love, and stand,
  Paying a price, at his right hand?
             (33–60)

In the *Monthly Repository* Browning attached an epigraph from Defoe's *Dictionary of all Religions* (1704) to the poem, and it included this sentence: 'Antinomians, so denominated for rejecting the Law as a thing of no use under Gospel dispensation.' (After 1842, Browning dropped this headnote.) As a sect, Antinomians stood, as their title suggests, against names. They would not be dictated to by any secular or religious institution. This point accentuates the obvious paradox at the heart of the poem. As Herbert F. Tucker observes: 'It is the dilemma of the Antionomian apologist . . . to have put into language a doctrine that sets itself against language, against the name, against the law and the problematics of interpretation.'[23] Supremely confident that he 'will get to God' (6), Agricola opens up his discourse while gazing at the stars, imagining himself to stand at a heavenly distance from 'hell's fierce bed'. As this sublime metaphor develops, so too does the magnanimity of his vision, Agricola taking on the privileged prospect of the God to whom he gives his praise. His language betrays the sincerity of his high-minded spiritual beliefs. The final lines expose his trust in God as a sham. Here the dominant register concerns economic transactions: 'warrant', 'reckon', 'bargain', 'price'. This highly materialistic vocabulary opposes the natural image of organic growth he uses at the start of the poem to represent how he has flourished under God's tender care: 'having thus created me, / Thus rooted me, he bade me grow, / Guiltless for ever, like a tree / That buds and blooms, nor seeks to know / The law by which it prospers so' (21–5). This is a revealingly illogical assertion. How can a religion predicated on an ignorance of the law it serves manage to define itself as a religion? His closing rhetorical question, therefore, looks all the more absurd. Although Agricola asks how he could praise God if he was able to 'reckon on' divine 'ways', he has already done so in order to postulate this question. The poem probes Agricola's spirited irrationality, drawing detailed attention to discrepancies between what is said and what is meant. It is as if this monologue were disclosing Agricola's unconscious motivation – exposing him as one whose language may reveal more than he is fully aware of, and who is thus attempting to live under the illusion of a dangerous fiction.

This noticeable gap between surface meaning and unconscious implication is the key characteristic of the monologue. E. Warwick Slinn notes that in this kind of poetry there is a 'breakdown' or 'ironic gap between self-expression and self-understanding',[24] while Tucker remarks on its pedagogical utility: 'As a sampling of dozens of poetry textbooks published in recent decades will confirm, the dramatic monologue is our genre of genres for training in how to read between the lines.'[25] Reading the monologue often means reading the language of the poem against itself – turning its rhetoric inside out to glimpse what the speaker may, unconsciously or not, be trying to conceal from view.

'Porphyria's Lover' operates in a similar manner to its companion piece, 'Johannes Agricola in Meditation'. Taking the same format (sixty octosyllabic lines), this monologue likewise opens up an ironic disjunction between statement and meaning but the poem is much more complex where the issue of motivation is concerned. Like Agricola, Porphyria's lover intuits a supposedly natural course of action that is, on inspection, illogical. Where Agricola rejects the authority of the Gospels, Porphyria's lover breaks God's law by perpetrating a murder. Echoing the name of the hero in Keats's 'The Eve of St Agnes' (1820), which contains a mysterious sexual encounter between Porphyro and Madeline, 'Porphyria's Lover' shares something of the Gothic interior of the earlier erotic poem. (The title also, it is worth noting, alludes to a physiological condition – porphyria refers to congenital abnormalities in pigmentation. In this context, the term suggests a link between physical and mental disease.) The opening runs very smoothly, chiefly because of the conjunction 'and' placed at the beginning of fifteen (a quarter) of the lines. Throughout, the poem achieves a remarkably even tone. Little may we think, at first, that this lover is a homicide. Even when describing the eerie storm outside that 'did its worst to vex the lake' (4), he sounds perfectly sane. If readers are particularly watchful, then the 'Elm-tops', signalling death, and which have been 'torn down for spite' (3) will presage Porphyria's terrible fate. Moreover, the storm outside bears some correspondence with the mental disorder that provokes the lover. Yet, while observing this violently animated nature, the lover's speech proceeds clearly and logically, so that these disturbing details only take on their full significance in retrospect. Spurious rationality governs the poem's deceptively easeful movement. Just as Agricola uses propositional clauses that establish a false sense of causality and motivation ('For in God's breast, my own abode' (8), 'For as I lie, smiled on, full-fed' (42)), the lover moves from thought to action in a manner that strikes him as perfectly reasonable. His narrative – frequently couched in words of one syllable only – enumerates Porphyria's every move and look in a carefully controlled manner. She performs the function of the perfect angel in the house. Gliding into the cottage, where the lover waits, her first action is to set the hearth ablaze, and this rekindling of the fire serves as a commonplace figure for the lover's aroused desires. They are, ostensibly, the perfect couple. But his desire is dulled by a syntax that would seem to lend equal weight to every idea, event, or object he itemises – whether it is her sensuous body (which he catalogues precisely: 'arm' (16), 'waist' (16), 'shoulder' (17), and 'hair' (18)) or the 'thing' he proposes to 'do' (38). Welcoming Porphyria's 'passion' (23, 26) and her 'worship' (33) of him, which he responds to with 'surprise' (34), he debates his course of action:

> That moment she was mine, mine, fair,
>   Perfectly pure and good: I found
> A thing to do, and all her hair
>   In one long yellow string I wound
>   Three times her little throat around
> And strangled her.
>
> (36–41)

At this pivotal point in the poem, it becomes clear for the first time that the lover is recounting, step by step, the history of a sexual murder. Once the denouement steals upon the closing lines, it is shockingly apparent that this is a very recent event since he now rests against Porphyria's corpse. Dramatic and temporal perspectives are subtly skewed by a shift in tense:

I propped her head up as before,
  Only, this time my shoulder bore
Her head, which droops upon it still:
  The smiling rosy little head,
So glad it has her utmost will,
  That all it scorned at once is fled,
  And I, its love, am gained instead!
Porphyria's love.

(49–55)

Slippages in grammar and word use are conspicuous here. Although the speaker first mentions 'her head', he swiftly impersonalises the pronoun so that Porphyria transmutes before his eyes into an inanimate thing – an 'it'. She becomes a property – something 'gained'. The richly ambiguous phrase 'I, its love, am gained instead' reveals how the identities of Porphyria and her lover have been merged in his mind. Even if the verb 'gained' appears passive in mood, it is also hintingly active in this suggestive construction. His will 'gains' hers but it is a 'gain' achieved only through a paradoxical annulment. As in Agricola's specious testimony, an economic metaphor tellingly intrudes upon this speaker's words. Emotional gain is conflated with material possession. Yet nothing has been 'gained' except a lifeless body. His speech concludes with his equivocal contemplation of the empty silence in which 'God has not said a word' (60). He anticipates – or at least has been anticipating – God's judgement. This may, on the one hand, strike a note of comfortless expectation. On the other, we may choose to think that the lover is expressing his relief at escaping God's wrath. It is hard to decide between these strongly divergent readings. And it is the undecideability of his final state of mind that prompts the reader to consider closely the brief and appallingly violent history that constitutes the poem. What exactly has driven him to do this deed?

There is no easy answer to this question. All that remains

clear is the trick the poem has played upon our sympathies. In the light of Fox's Benthamite poetics, it might be said that both of these 'Madhouse Cells', as the two poems were named in *Dramatic Lyrics*, reveal spontaneous actions or intuitions as extremely worrying. Even though Agricola and Porphyria's lover adopt an argumentative form of reasoning, they betray the rational mind by acting on impulse – to selfish ends. Their pleasures are not for the greatest number but for themselves alone. Needless to say, both are deranged. For each, self-aggrandisement is the prominent feature of the crazed mind. And it might be argued that both poems take one of the central preoccupations of Romantic aesthetics to their potentially most devastating ends. If Romanticism redefined the perception of the world through the active projection of the individual will – so that the subject creates the object through, say, the faculty of the imagination – then it may well follow that the subject is in jeopardy of hallucinating reality. Perhaps one way of understanding the dangers of Romanticism is through Keats's well-known jibe at Wordsworth's apparent indulgence in the 'egotistical sublime'. Overemphasis on the self can, as we see here, lead to the annihilation of the other, particularly where sexual pleasure is concerned. (Romanticism, after all, in its wider eighteenth-century European context, produced the work of the Marquis de Sade – the most extensive body of material on sexual violence and power from the period.) Porphyria's lover assumes that she adores him at the moment when he is able to believe that all her 'pride, and vainer ties' (24) – her sense of individual will, and her connection with other individuals – have been broken. A great number of Browning's monologues would hereafter concentrate on the problem of the limits to individual freedom, and how and why individualism was necessary in a society searching for broader forms of democracy between the classes and the sexes. As a consequence, middle-class intellectuals were becoming much more sensitive to the way in which individual rights might be abused.

In his essay on 'Browning and the dramatic monologue', Michael Mason investigates 'Porphyria's Lover' from two other standpoints – first, as a poem emerging from the inhospitable conditions for stage drama; and second, as a poem attentive to early nineteenth-century writings on psychiatry (notably, the writings of J. E. D. Esquirol). The fact that 'legitimate' drama could only be performed at the 'patent' theatres of Covent Garden and Drury Lane obviously enforced a severe restriction on the development of early Victorian theatre, and so it is possible to see the emergence of dramatic poetry as a response to that crisis. As Mason points out, there were numerous scripts of 'unacted' dramas in circulation.[26] Browning, of course, had aspirations to the stage, and his first tragedy, concerning Strafford's impeachment, was performed in London in 1837. It was variously praised and derided, achieving a short run – certainly not the type of theatrical success he had anticipated.

Like the two 'Madhouse Cells', Browning's plays show fascination with questions of power, especially its use and abuse in the hands of statesmen. These were ambitious works. *Luria* (1845), for example, is implicitly a revision of *Othello*, interrogating the manipulation of an African general leading Florentine armies against Pisa. The main trouble with these dramas was their tortuous plotting, and this made them hard to follow on stage. Although Browning's avowed aim, as he stated in the Preface to *Strafford*, was to animate 'Action in Character rather than Character in Action',[27] the complex equivocations about the handling of power that affect almost every one of his heroes largely went over the heads of his theatre audience. The political orientation of his poems would have been much clearer to his readers. *Dramatic Lyrics*, for example, opens with three rousing 'Cavalier Tunes', which, as George Bornstein notes, send up the monarchism enshrined in the bicentennial celebrations of the Civil War that were taking place when Browning's pamphlet was published in 1842.[28] These 'cavalier' songs obviously echo the concerns of *Strafford*, and drive at the heart of those questions of democracy arising from the factionalism that pitched Cromwell against the Crown.

In a detailed account of the early poems and plays, John Woolford usefully refers to Browning's uneasy attraction to questions of governance as an *'embarrassment at power'*. Woolford sees this as 'the central problem for a humanist of Browning's type', and he notes three recurring motifs in the poet's writings of the 1830s and 1840s: *'apostasy* – specifically, apostasy from liberal causes; *abdication* from political power; and the *resumption* or *arrogation* of political power after abdication'.[29] The plays cannot be analysed at length in this discussion. All that needs to be noted is that each examines the moral dilemmas experienced by those who know how to govern by right principles and yet recognise that state power corrupts. This problem sounds the keynote of *King Victor and King Charles* (1842) where a despotic father (Victor) abdicates, foisting the rule of Sardinia upon his reluctant son (Charles), only to discover that Charles finds the responsibilities of government unbearable, and so the crown reverts to the unsympathetic father who had given it away in the first place. One general point about Browning's work should be apparent here. Taken together, the plays, the early narrative poems, and the short dramatic lyrics demonstrate a considerable anxiety about human agency. If the Romantic period, ignited by the ambitions of 1789, asserted the primacy of individual rights (liberty, equality and fraternity), the bourgeois Browning, rummaging for examples from history books and psychiatric studies, clearly recognised that power was a very precarious instrument and that its effects were all too frequently misapprehended.

The dramatic lyric proved to be his most enduring form for exploring the dynamics of power because it contextualised the history it was dealing with concisely and so had a more immediate impact on his readers than the plays. It is now commonplace to explain the dramatic monologue according to the formula laid out by Robert Langbaum in his very influential study, *The Poetry of Experience* (1957), since it is there that he establishes a general rule for our response to the rhetorical seductiveness of those speakers whose words we must finally reject as unacceptable. Sympathy comes first. Judgement soon follows. This procedure is followed by both of Browning's original 'Madhouse Cells'. Epitomising some of the characteristic emphases on formal qualities laid down by the American New Criticism (with its interest in tension, ambiguity and paradox), Langbaum argues that the distinct 'modernity' of the dramatic monologue derives from its questioning attitude towards universal truths:

> it is precisely the modern condition that there is no publicly accepted moral and emotional Truth, there are only perspectives towards it – those partial meanings which individuals may get a glimpse of at particular moments but which, formulated as ideas for other moments and people, become problematical. The empiricism of the dramatic monologue, as demonstrated by its disequilibrium between sympathy and judgement, is a sign that imitates not life but a particular perspective towards life, somebody else's experience of it.[30]

Langbaum argues that experience is not an *a priori* given in the monologue. Experience, instead, is a construction, and its value varies according to the interpretative 'perspective' brought to bear on it. Such poetry, unlike eighteenth-century writing, is not concerned with 'imitating . . . nature or an order of ideas about nature but the structure of experience itself' (p. 40). This general point is borne out by Langbaum's highly attentive reading of 'My Last Duchess', a poem which has proved to be something of a test case for comprehending the operations of the monologue, and the dual movement of sympathy and judgement forms the centre of his critical analysis. Initially identifying with the speaker, the reader is eventually alienated from the words that have been overheard. Hypothesising the reader's response to the Duke in 'My Last Duchess', Langbaum asserts: 'We suspend moral judgement because we prefer to participate in the Duke's power and freedom, in his hard core of character fiercely loyal to itself. Moral judgement is in fact important as the thing to be suspended, as a measure of the price we pay for the privilege of appreciating to the full this extraordinary man' (p. 77). Yet this model can only describe a general tendency in the dramatic monologue to draw the reader into an active relationship with the poem. In 'My Last Duchess', there are several sympathies and forms of judgement awaiting investigation, and these do not fit squarely together.

Critics have been remarkably at variance when analysing the Duke's motivation. In this poem, the Duke (loosely modelled on Alfonso II, Duke of Ferrara) addresses the envoy of a less wealthy family than his own to negotiate the dowry for his future marriage to an unidentified young noblewoman. In the process he draws aside a curtain to expose Frà Pandolf's greatly prized painting of his last Duchess. Gradually, it becomes clear that there were aspects of her personality which irritated him so profoundly that he saw fit to murder her – probably by using hired assassins. All of this is couched in the Duke's carefully controlled rhetoric. The Duke, an especially adept speaker, fills Langbaum with admiration: 'What interests us more than the Duke's wickedness is his immense attractiveness. His conviction of matchless superiority, his intelligence and bland amorality, his taste for art, his manners . . . these qualities overwhelm the envoy . . . The reader is no less overwhelmed' (p. 77). Envoy and reader, then, are placed in a similar position.

Yet how can this be the case? One is directly addressed; the other eavesdrops. Although Langbaum states that the monologue constructs multiple perspectives towards truth, his notion of sympathy would seem to collapse these differences of view under a single harmonising law. There are other inconsistencies in the theory laid out in *The Poetry of Experience*. In his essay 'The dramatic monologue and related lyric forms', Ralph W. Rader objects to Langbaum's reasoning where the Duke's motivation is concerned. Langbaum argues that the Duke discloses his true identity accidentally: 'The Duchess's goodness shines through the Duke's utterance; he makes no attempt to conceal it, so preoccupied is he with his own standard of judgement and so oblivious to the world's' (p. 78). Rader observes that 'Langbaum is typical of critics when he sees the Duke as not up to much of anything', stressing that 'the Duke reveals himself with deliberate calculation, for a specific purpose'.[31] And this remark repeats the differences of opinion between earlier critics, one of whom found the Duke 'witless', and another who thought him 'shrewd'.[32] Where Langbaum sees the Duke's motives exposed by chance, Rader considers them wholly purposeful. Why, then, has the Duke's speech led to these entirely opposed conclusions? What is it that gives rise to such ambiguity?

Intentionality occupies Tucker's far reaching analysis of 'My Last Duchess', implying that both Langbaum and Rader have identified differing qualities present in the poem. He helpfully shifts the debate about the poem away from the rights and wrongs of the Duke's empirical character on to issues of language and representation. Although critics recognise the disparity between statement and meaning, it is *what* is betrayed that keeps them in dispute. Tucker performs a useful act of reconciliation here, and it is valuable to trace, and extend, his reading. He begins by noting the internal divisions within the Duke's speech. Systematically interrupting his discourse, the Duke gestures towards his supposedly inadequate locutions: 'how shall I say' (22), 'I know not how' (32), and, most tellingly, 'skill/In speech – (which I have not) – ' (35–6). Each has a double effect. On the one hand, they express

modesty, attempting to control the impression made upon the
envoy. On the other, given their recurrence, they suggest the
Duke's discomfort, even paranoia. Tucker notes: 'when a
skilled rhetorician reaches three times for the same commonplace . . . the commonplace is no longer common but the
expression of a private struggle'.[33] While in the process of
trying to make his mark, he has an anxious compulsion to
repeat. It would seem as if the Duke were wrestling with a
language whose power to signify is troublingly greater than
his own. The more the poem unravels, with its unsettling
phrasing, the more Tucker is able to tease out the Duke's
considerable discursive unease: 'The Duke is the heir of a
heavily traditional sense of himself' – possessing a highly valued
'nine-hundred-years-old name' (33) – 'which prescribes fixed
relations between form and meaning'.[34] The trouble is, the
Duke begins to cast doubt on the values he espouses, almost in
spite of himself. As he discloses more about his 'last Duchess'
(sounding, chillingly, as though she was one of a series), her
portrait lovingly executed by Frà Pandolf, and her sudden death,
the wider the gap opens between intention and meaning. This
point becomes even more complex since the poem makes
intentionality a thematic, as well as rhetorical, concern.

'My Last Duchess' draws attention to a disjunction between
verbal 'skill' and intent or 'will':

> Even had you skill
> In speech – (which I have not) – to make your will
> Quite clear to such an one, and say, 'Just this
> Or that in you disgusts me: here you miss,
> Or there exceed the mark' – and if she let
> Herself be lessoned so, nor plainly set
> Her wits to yours, forsooth, and made excuse
> – E'en then would be some stooping; and I choose
> Never to stoop.
> (35–43)

There is a blatant irony here. Although the Duke makes his will (or intention) clear, he none the less chooses to deny this in a deftly inserted parenthesis. Moreover, even though 'will' supposedly requires 'skill/In speech', the fact that these words fit together in a quietened rhyme neatly accomplishes what he claims is deficient in his speech. His will, whether he likes it or not, is framed by the intent of the poem. There is, then, a way of understanding how the speaker and the poem are articulating contrary meanings. It might be said that the Duke's lyric will is undermined by the dramatic structure that frames his words. Another way of phrasing this would be to say that the *written* quality of the poem supersedes the *speech* it contains. As Eric Griffiths suggests, the dramatic monologue serves an ambivalent function, as a 'printed voice', where the spoken and written levels mark out differences of timing, as well as tone.[35]

'My Last Duchess', therefore, concentrates on exposing competing interpretations between the Duke's will and his skill (or lack of it) to represent his intentions, and its skill at doing the same. His rhetorical discomfiture deepens considerably when he reveals himself unable to decode the intentions of others. All the characters in the short history he adumbrates – himself, the Duchess, and Frà Pandolf – have desires and demands that he chooses to regard in a damagingly restrictive manner. Since, according to Tucker, 'the poem establishes a set of relationships between reader and text, Duke and painting', the poem may be understood as 'a study in the reductive study of poetry'; he compares the Duke (with perhaps slight condescension) to the literary 'student impatient of uncertainties that would fix the meaning of a text beyond doubt'.[36] Given that the Duke prides himself on his capacity to 'read' (6) Frà Pandolf's picture, 'My Last Duchess' certainly suggests that it may read as a poem about interpretative procedures, and how we may adjudicate between varying ones. In fact, the poem is, among other things, built around a series of readings – the Duke of the painting; the painter of the

Duchess; the Duke of the painter; and so on. Each interpretative structure ironises the other. As in 'Porphyria's Lover', the speaker recounts a past event to account for the present time of action. Here, the time of remembrance and the living present coincide in Frà Pandolf's much admired portrait of the Duchess. The picture, which the Duke usually keeps veiled, brings the Duchess alive for him. Doubtless Pandolf's skills produced a very accurate likeness of her. Although the Duke treasures the art work as one of his most prized objects, he abhors the woman represented there. Yet, once her face has been uncurtained, there is something in the 'depth and passion' of her penetratingly 'earnest glance' (8) that disquiets him. His gaze attempts to estimate hers. And so the poem discloses the important difference between them.

Addressing the envoy, the Duke accuses his late wife of sexual scandal. He believes she was conducting an affair, not only with Frà Pandolf, but also other men on his estate:

> Sir, 'twas not
> Her husband's presence only, called that spot
> Of joy into the Duchess' cheek: perhaps
> Frà Pandolf chanced to say 'Her mantle laps
> Over my lady's wrist too much', or 'Paint
> Must never hope to reproduce the faint
> Half-flush that dies along her throat': such stuff
> Was courtesy, she thought, and cause enough
> For calling up that spot of joy. She had
> A heart – how shall I say? – too soon made glad,
> Too easily impressed; she liked whate'er
> She looked on, and her looks went everywhere.
> Sir, 'twas all one!
>   (13–25)

It should be obvious that he is misreading Frà Pandolf's compliments in the very act of quoting him. Where the Duke reduces the artist's intentions to lasciviousness, Frà Pandolf's kindly words focus on the inadequacy of art to reproduce the original it copies. The painter, it seems, recognises that there is inevitably a space between the two, and that no amount of artistic skill will bring them together. For the modest Pandolf, the Duchess's splendid 'spot of joy' cannot appear in paint, although it would appear that his talent as a painter is much greater than he himself would admit. For the 'spot of joy' is surely there – perfectly replicated. It radiates from the picture, making the Duchess seem 'as if she were alive' (2). If sympathy is to be located anywhere in this poem, it must ultimately be with her, and with the 'looks' she may well have given generously (not sexually) to her admirers.

The Duchess's 'spot of joy' is irrepressible. Although her 'faint half-flush' is for the Duke exclusively a glaring sign of her adultery (it 'dies', in a cruelly punning way, 'along her throat'), it is more likely than not for Frà Pandolf a sign of her exquisite complexion. Likewise, although this 'spot' is for the Duke the smear or blot on her reputation, it is the distinctive mark of her joyful and generous presence for all the other men in her life. While the Duke tries to close in on one interpretation, justifying his annihilation of her, his language contains within it entirely contrary suggestions – that the Duchess was well loved by her servants; that she did not respect him simply because he was a member of an ancient family. His strongly connotative words indicate that even when she was 'lessoned' (40) (told off, put in her place), she also 'lessened' him, since he found that she had her 'wits' (41) about her, and with great charm she politely challenged his rude authority. Constantly maintaining her grace (she accepts Frà Pandolf's praise as 'courtesy' (20)), and captivating everyone's attention with her lovable 'smile' (45), the Duchess would not be treated badly by him, and so he had to 'stoop' (43) to recover his dignity. This, by inference, is the subtext to his account.

The 'spot' is a remarkable figuration. It is the central site of interpretation here, and the poem draws up various perspectives around it. Even though the Duke tries to veil the 'spot', he is compelled to reveal it – it still has a hold on his mind, and it proves to be the magnetic source at the centre of the poem. As Loy D. Martin states, 'the triumph of Browning's poem lies in the way it prevents its readers from repeating the Duke's error'.[37] Since 'My Last Duchess' actively encourages varying responses to the incidents recounted by the Duke, a much more relativistic approach to truth would seem to emerge. And that is Langbaum's original point. Yet, even if the truth of the Duchess' behaviour turns out to be subject to multiple points of view, and thus to dispute, one thing is for sure: the Duke is in the wrong. The poem has a moral to make, and, on analysis, it exercises a concealed form of jurisdiction. It, too, has its intentions. But the power issuing from the poem, if standing over and against the Duke's, is different in kind. The poem serves to correct the Duke's attitude towards language, implying a much more open way of thinking about the world and its meanings. Although the Duke is a skilful rhetorician, the poem is more so – since it works within a negativity or ironic space that knows that words will resist any closure upon them. 'My Last Duchess', then, would seem to be in full grasp of the knowledge of itself as an allegory of interpretation.

The poem, therefore, has a metapoetic quality to it. The main device it uses to address its own status as an interpretative form is irony. And irony is the key trope of internal differentiation. Irony involves distancing language from itself. In an important essay on the structuring figures within traditions of European Romanticism, Paul de Man argues that irony accompanies moments of reflection, whereby the material stuff of language is separated out from the world it seeks to represent. Quoting Charles Baudelaire's essay on the essence of laughter, de Man observes that for artists language has a distinctive status: 'language is their material, just as leather is the material of the cobbler or wood is that of the carpenter', and he continues:

In everyday, common existence, this is not how language usually operates; there it functions much more as does the cobbler's or the carpenter's hammer, not as the material itself, but as a tool by means of which the heterogeneous material of experience is more or less adequately made to fit. The reflective disjunction not only occurs *by means of* language as a privileged category, but it transfers the self out of the empirical world into a world constituted out of, and in, language – a language that it finds in the world among one entity among others, but that remains unique in being the only entity means of which it can differentiate itself from the world. Language thus conceived divides the subject into an empirical self, immersed in the world, and a self that becomes like a sign in its attempt at differentiation and self-definition. [38]

There are, then, two selves which emerge from the moment of ironic reflection: one which sees itself as the agent of representation, and another that is consigned to the form of representation itself. As a consequence, the very concept of the self is divided. Exploiting irony, Browning's poetry often seems to want to overmaster it – to bring irony within the compass of the knowledge that it, as poetry, is producing. Yet if irony continually subverts claims to mastery (such as the Duke's), how can any poem come into possession of the 'reflective disjunction' that irony prises apart? This is the special preoccupation of many of Browning's poems which struggle to interpret the impossibility of direct and decisive communication between the self and the world it inhabits.

Given de Man's examples of the cobbler and the carpenter, it would seem advisable at this point to return to the material world which is now problematically viewed through the split lens of irony. Two points may be raised here about the historical condition of this ironised self. John Lucas remarks that 'My Last Duchess' poses 'the connection between "sophisticated" aristocracy and oppressive, even murderous, patriarchy',[39] pointing out that Browning's links with the *Monthly Repository* brought the poet into contact with women writers who continued the work of Mary Wollstonecraft. Women contributors to the journal were explicitly feminist, and traces of their critique can surely be felt in this poem – and possibly in 'Porphyria's Lover' too. (It is no accident that Fox introduced John Stuart Mill and Harriet Taylor to one another.) The strongly Dissenting, middle-class element of 'My Last Duchess' appears in its final moment where the Duke turns to another of his art treasures. As if making an instructive example, he says:

> Notice Neptune, though,
> Taming a sea-horse, thought a rarity,
> Which Claus of Innsbruck cast in bronze for me!
> (54–6)

These lines draw up a disconcerting parallel between the Duke and Neptune, both of whom attempt to tame those with less power. Just as the Duchess has refused to submit, so too does the poem seem to be resisting aristocratic authority. That such power should be attributed to an art work 'thought a rarity' makes his arrogant desires all the more hypocritical. For those, like Browning, influenced by Utilitarian and subsequent liberal thought, art has a different function. For one thing, it seeks to indicate the errors of others in the name of greater individual freedom. The Duke, a rich man, grossly abuses his position. And this observation points to a political tension within Browning's ironic poetics.

Liberalism, in its classic formulation, focuses on the limits of toleration to safeguard individual freedoms. Although everyone has the right to be an individual, no individual has the right to stop someone else from being so: this is the guiding precept of liberal doctrine. Devising constraints and checks on power to maintain this balance proves enduringly difficult, and it follows that many people subscribing to 'liberal' values range very widely across the political spectrum. In Victorian Britain, liberalism defined an exceptionally elastic set of values. It would bring minds as distinct, and opposed, as Browning and the poet and critic, Matthew Arnold, under the same banner. Yet it was not as inclusive as it may have liked to have been. Aiming to keep everybody's differences in abeyance as much as possible, liberal ethics assumed that areas of debate where conflict may be ignited should be carefully circumscribed, if not banished from view. At the risk of generalisation, it can be said that this tension between the competing rights of contending political opinions meant that Victorian liberal culture, which was overwhelmingly middle class, gave more prominence to the complexity of the individual than to class dissension. Psychology frequently superseded explicit politics.

This is the case with Browning's poetry, and middle-class Victorian poetry as a whole. It is also a pronounced tendency in the reviews of poetry published in the 1830s and 1840s. A good example of the hostility to politics in bourgeois poetry is Coventry Patmore's response to Tennyson's Maud (1855), a poem in which the deranged protagonist blusters towards a jingoistic ending praising the virtues of the Crimean War: 'The fever of politics should not have been caught by the Laureate, even under the disguise of a monomaniac'.[40] Even when framed as an exposé of madness (Tennyson probed the crazed mind just as deeply as – if differently from – Browning), Maud proved distasteful because it put forward a point of view about current affairs. Tennyson was not being eccentric here; the disastrous war of 1854–6 galvanised a huge amount of support for the military. Alan Sinfield notes that even the writings of Fox, one of the most radical writers of his day, place far more emphasis on the mind than the material world:

In the context of Fox's argument, it can be seen that what is being offered to poetry is the space which is left when the main business of the world has been done elsewhere. Shelley's claim to address the most important human issues – the way a whole society functions – is disallowed: imaginative freedom and political freedom are split apart, and to poetry is left 'states of mind'. This strategy resembles both relegation and incorporation, but it is nevertheless distinct: poetry is a valued part of the utilitarian world so long as it does not intrude on the real conditions of life. It is *marginalized*. [41]

At a time when a great deal of clearly political poetry was being written by, for, and about the workers – such as Ebenezer Elliott's *Corn-Law Rhymes* (1830), which Fox admired[42] – middle-class poets were gradually dissociating themselves from the body of the people, and turning to the intriguing mental irregularities of the individual.

Reviewing the achievements of Victorian poetry in 1893, the socialist Henry Salt wrote in his introduction to an anthology of political verse:

> it is a remarkable fact, and worth a trifle more consideration than critics are disposed to afford it, that neither Tennyson nor Browning, neither our great 'representative' poet, nor our great 'intellectual' poet, was cognisant of the real drift of the social movement that dates from the stormy years of the 'Forties' [namely, Chartism]. [43]

To answer this charge, it is inappropriate, if tempting, to suggest that Browning's interest in the Hungry Forties and the Crimean War in the 1850s was diminished by the fact he lived for fifteen years in Italy. It is certainly true that passing references to contemporary political struggles are scattered very sparsely in his writing of this time. And, indeed, the lack of reference to current affairs characterises most bourgeois poetry between 1830 and 1890. In *Bells and Pomegranates* there is a momentary allusion to the Corn Laws, one of the main campaigning platforms for working people, in 'The Englishman in Italy' (1845), where the speaker treats this contentious legislation with disapproval: 'if abolishing Corn Laws/Be righteous and wise/– If 'twere proper, Scirocco would vanish/In black from the skies' (289–92). Whether this is Browning's opinion or not is open to question. The dramatic structure of his work cautions against any easy conflation between poet and persona.

The point is, the political reference is less significant than the general tenor of the poem – which traces a tourist's light-hearted observations of another culture, estimating its difference from his own. Patrick Brantlinger notes that these lines, often cited as an instance of Browning's active liberal principles, were, in fact, added on as an afterthought (Elizabeth Barrett, who influenced the shape and design of many of the poems in *Dramatic Romances and Lyrics*, felt the lines improved the unity of the poem as a whole): 'the tacked-on ending of "The Englishman in Italy" expresses guilt for Browning's own political inertia as well as anger at tariffs and also at politics generally'.[44] The charge of 'political inertia' is somewhat too harsh. To understand Browning's liberalism one has to see how its often uneasy thoughts about power are displaced from the contemporary scene into other poetic spaces. In most of Browning's shorter poems the immediate concerns of the everyday Victorian world are less prominent than those of the past, and his work is frequently drawn to ostensibly alien worlds. Protestant nineteenth-century England frequently looks back to fifteenth-century Roman Catholic Italy. But Browning's retrospective – apparently turning its gaze to other cultures and other times – is not a complete deflection from the class struggles mounting in Victorian Britain. As his 'Cavalier Tunes' demonstrate, the past bore witness to present conflicts: 1642 addresses 1842. The Civil War is a reference point for Chartism. Browning's politics are to be found, then, not in the contemporary world, but through the filter of history, and the analysis of historical processes.

This apparent lack of interest in 'real conditions' (unionisation; public demonstrations; and other direct challenges to capitalist authority) distinguishes Browning's poetry as very much of its class and culture. It is, unmistakably, a bourgeois poetry. To be 'bourgeois', etymologically, meant to be a freeman or freeburgher. And it is to the exploration of that freedom seeking subjectivity that his poetry turns. Each of the poems examined here – the 'Madhouse Cells' and 'My Last Duchess' – forms part of a poetry attempting to understand how the self constitutes itself, its consciousness no less, in history. And each poem, in turn, reveals this to be a problematic affair. The monologue is a historically structured form since the 'I' that speaks must provide the time, manner and place of its own speaking. Duty bound to contextualise itself, the monologue must bespeak the conditions of its own speaking. Yet placing the 'I' in historical context is not simply a matter of asserting a wholly autonomous self, for it is in these poetic acts of self-constitution that psychological conflicts arise, and with them differences of interpretation on how the 'I' perceives and is perceived in a world whose meanings are open to ironic reflection. Lucas believes that the multiplicity of perspectives enabled by irony make Browning's writing democratic.[45] Only, one might add, in so far as it is, in its specifically Victorian way, *liberal*, since the democracy enabled by irony always has, at the end, a place of independent authority from which to reflect on the world, and distance the self from it. All in all, the monologue situates, at its core, a position from which the errors of others may be historically accounted for and judged.

That said, judgement is never final – it remains suspended, in the ambience of reflection, and the peculiarity of mind. Motivation remains throughout a problem, and it is never known for sure, since it is altogether too complex. Which is to say that although the unethical *results* of his speakers' actions may be clear, the *causes* are much less so. Liberalism is forever obliged to permit some leeway to everyone's own peculiar point of view, even if they are – as is often the case – in the wrong. That is why Agricola, Porphyria's lover and the Duke are allowed their hearings, and so invite the reader's speculations. It is the least a middle-class poet may do for the individual.

3

Histories and Historicism

The nineteenth century was the age of historicism, and J. Hillis Miller has remarked that the 'dramatic monologue is par excellence the literary genre of historicism'. He adds:

> It presupposes a double awareness on the part of the author, an awareness which is the very essence of historicism. The dramatic monologuist is aware of the relativity, the arbitrariness of any single life or way of looking at the world.[1]

But what exactly is this arbitrariness that defines historicism? For the Victorians, very generally, it meant that history was *interpretable* and, in that, an *interpretative device* for higher forms of knowledge. In other words, historical researches were becoming as significant as those of philosophy. Peter Allen Dale sums up the main tendencies of historicism as follows:

> The first thing to be noted about nineteenth-century historicism is that it began by setting up historical process not as in itself a sufficient explanation of experience but as the most likely venue to

such an explanation. Not through physics or metaphysics could one best discover the meaning of life, but through history. For the theistically or idealistically inclined this meant that history became the revelation of God's or Absolute Spirit's providential design for mankind. For the more positivistically inclined, history was nothing so magical as a revelation, but it was, nonetheless, a very important key to the meaning of life.[2]

In its early nineteenth-century beginnings, historicism enabled thinkers to devise a means of understanding how civilisations progressed within a theological framework. Carried to extremes, in later years, it meant that all historical processes were viewed as exclusively human phenomena – without telos or divine purpose.

Although history has always been subject to claims and counter-claims as to its veracity, in the nineteenth century it was desperately plunged into controversy with the advent of new knowledges that threw fundamental doubt on former certainties. Each, in its own way, contributed to the diminishment of Christian faith. Geology (challenging biblical history); natural history and evolutionism (doing much the same); the biblical Higher Criticism (questioning the authenticity of the Gospels): all these innovative methods for comprehending the formation of the world – either through volcanic eruptions, natural selection or story telling devices – finally wrested it from God's hands and placed it among processes that, on the one hand, stretched back into prehistory, before the written or spoken word, and, on the other, pointed to the duplicities of historiography – the written material which records what has gone before. Whether they liked it or not, the Victorians were becoming painfully aware of a range of *temporalities* and *narratives*, and these undermined the clarity of human origins that once had been taken for granted. They were gripped by the idea of history – not just its content, but the representational forms it took.

Above all, understanding how and why history relied on varying interpretations of written records became a deeply problematical affair, especially in relation to Christianity. Browning's casuistical poems on biblical topics (the raising of Lazarus; the vision of Saul; St Paul's first mission; and so on) directly engage with the polemical writings of David Friedrich Strauss and Ernest Renan, whose Higher Criticism of the New Testament, in distinct but allied ways, flew in the face of theological orthodoxies. Both critics explored variances between the Gospels. Browning, although ready to admit the ever wavering circumstances of historical documentation, could not take their critiques of the authenticity of Matthew, Mark, Luke and especially John on trust. In fact, Strauss's and Renan's writings on the questionable status of St John's Gospel provoked him into a spirited defence of Christian history that did not depend, for its value, on the Bible as a narrative of unassailable truth.

This was an unusual manoeuvre for a Victorian to make. In his poems on the Higher Criticism, he brings the voices of biblical figures alive, allowing them to argue the case that historical facticity need not be the guarantor of Christian belief. Nineteenth-century creations, his biblical personae are projected into the past to converse with the present. Their words are full of indirect but cautionary reminders about how to preserve one's faith in a time of spiritual crisis. By creating his own New Testament fictions – such as St John's death-bed speech – Browning is demonstrating that faith is not contingent on whether or not we can or should prove the miracles performed by Christ, and on which the Higher Critics cast so much doubt. Instead, it is the power of fiction making – the spiritual efficacy of creativity itself – that informed his Christianity. By all accounts, Browning was turning the arguments of the Higher Critics back on themselves since he found a way of drawing their methodology into Christianity, not away from it.

The Higher Criticism, which produced some of the most radical challenges of nineteenth-century historicism, was accommodated within his religious aesthetic. And each phase of the historical process was for him part of a divine plan, not in any predestinarian sense, but as an evolving process. God's historical outline was viewed as progressive and developmental, and the progress of artistic forms, from one era to another, bore witness to this truth. But, of course, an account of history such as this could not reach a point where it dispensed with its prime mover. In no way was Browning able to accept the far reaching implications of Darwin's theory of 'natural selection', laid out in *The Origin of Species* (1859); he claimed, on one occasion, that Darwin's 'philosophy' was 'of little or no importance', although it was significant enough for him to dismiss it at length in a late poem.[3] When taxed on this issue, he declared that the general direction of Darwin's evolutionary model, available to him when he was in his late forties, was one he had already inferred for himself, and, more importantly still, one that belonged to an overall scheme laid out by God. He wrote in 1881:

about my being 'strongly against Darwin, rejecting the truths of science and regretting its advance' – you only do I should hope and expect in disbelieving *that* . . . In reality, all that seems *proved* in Darwin's scheme was a conception familiar to me from the beginning: see in *Paracelsus* the progressive development from senseless matter to organized, until man's appearance (Part V [V. 638–711]). Also in *Cleon*, see the order of 'life's mechanics' [202], – and I daresay in many passages of my poetry: for how can one look at Nature as a whole and doubt that, wherever there is a gap, a 'link' must be missing – through the limited power and opportunity of the looker? But go back and back, as you please . . . you find (*my* faith is constant) creative intelligence, acting as matter but not resulting from it. Once set the balls rolling, and ball may hit ball and send any number in any direction over the table; but I believe in the cue pushed by a hand. When one is taunted (as I notice is often fancied as an easy method with the un-Darwinized) – taunted with thinking successive acts of creation credible, metaphysics have been stopped short at, however physics may fare: time and space being purely conceptions of our own, wholly inapplicable to intelligence of another kind – with whom, as I made Luria say, there is an 'everlasting moment of creation' [*Luria* (1846), V. 233], if one at all, – past, present, and future, one and the same state. This consideration does not affect Darwinism proper in any degree. But I do not consider that his case as to the changes in organization, brought about by desire and will in the creature, is proved.[4]

From the outset, Browning could accept the gradual ascent of animal into human forms, just as he saw the history of civilisations as an eventual movement towards more advanced cultures. Yet in this letter he protests loudly that the Darwinian position presumes a God-like knowledge of the evolutionary process that no human being could reasonably make. He objects to the Darwinian hypothesis of the 'missing link' – joining primates and human beings – because it seeks to undermine the harmony of God's order. Against this, he sets his 'faith', and what he can infer from the evidences of the world – bound by space and time – around him. This extract shows that his understanding of Darwin was not particularly deep, since here he collapses a Lamarckian model of 'desire and will in the creature' into Darwin's work on 'natural selection'. (Popularisations of Darwin still confuse these two differing models to this day.) He remonstrates against the idea that animal desires and the human will can, for and in themselves, adapt to their environments, and thus transform species. It is God, not his creatures, that decides their shape and substance; while they express an inherited or governed desire for growth and development. Such remarks indicate that if Browning was avant-garde in the 1830s, he was, in some respects, behind his time fifty years later. There again, given his open-minded attitude to the fictive element in all historical knowledge, he was far less troubled than many of his contemporaries by its destabilising effects. In part this is because he had come into contact with German biblical hermeneutics well before most Victorians. Fox's *Monthly Repository* was perhaps the only journal to engage directly with the first manifestations of the German Higher Criticism in Britain.[5]

This chapter examines Browning's historicist poetry in relation to two distinct but related phases of culture: first, the Italian Renaissance; and second, the events immediately following Christ's incarnation. In both, Browning is identifying forms of divine revelation – in high art as well as Christ's miracles. And in both Browning finds it extremely difficult to handle the problems of metapoetic authority invested in the claims he is making about God's evolutionary plan. This is perhaps his major epistemological problem. For he has to take up a highly authoritative position, one set over against his personae, to indicate how and why he is correct, while they, more often than not, remain in error. His generous receptivity to the findings of the historicists is counter-weighted by his overinterpretive desire to impress the idea that his historical model, which is also God's, is the right one. At times, the liberal-minded Browning can haunt his speaker's voices in tones that verge on the dogmatic. Each poem under discussion here exposes the considerable tension that builds up between his interest in relativising human truth claims (allowing a variety of opinions; giving the individual freedom of speech; enabling irony to disrupt relations between intention and meaning) and a religious concern with encircling these ever contingent beliefs beneath an incontestable faith in divine truth (God's historical plan; the poet's privilege to reveal it; and its magnanimous capacity to absorb all objections to its unstoppable movement towards the millennium).

In scrutinising history and the interpretation of historical processes, Browning was participating in an activity shared by a very wide range of left- and right-wing intellectuals and artists. All kinds of cultural production in Victorian Britain reflected an obsessive concern with representing the past: to recapture and reimagine it, and so use it to draw up parallels with the present. Victorian painting, for example, is dominated by historical subjects: classical, medieval, Renaissance, and, particularly, British early modern. The turbulent 1830s were preoccupied with an earlier period of similar social discontent: galleries were filled with depictions of scenes from the English Civil War – the paintings of Daniel Maclise and Paul Dela-roche, in particular, come to mind. One era above all dominated the Victorian imagination, and that was the Middle Ages. The Gothic revival, at its peak in the 1840s, most prominently displays the groundswell of neo-medievalism, and it is fair to say that this style was the one upon which most Victorian poets seized.

But, where subject matter is concerned, Browning is in some important respects an anomaly here, since he did not choose to explore medieval styles and customs, and the pre-capitalist untaintedness they seemed to represent. The Gothic revival would appear to have been contaminated for him by the Roman Catholic resurgence of the 1840s, as 'Bishop Blou-gram's Apology' (1855) shows. There, Browning uses his arch-casuist, a wine quaffing bishop, to pontificate on the glories of 'preaching in basilicas, / And doing duty in some masterpiece / Like this of brother Pugin's' (5–7). Pugin, a Catholic convert, was the chief architect in the renewal of Gothic styles, and espoused political views that appealed to the more reactionary elements in Victorian society. 'Bishop Blougram's Apology' is a lively satirical attack on the reestablishment of the Catholic hierarchy in London. Despite Browning's rather disingenuous claims to the contrary, his speaker is modelled on noted members of the priesthood. He, like several commentators in the periodicals, associated Catholicism with bizarre forms of superstition, and so he made fun of the cheekily 'winking

Virgin' (377).[6] Yet his most mischievous ploy is to show how this bishop, revealing more than he might were he sober, does not really believe in all that he professes.

Elsewhere Browning mocks the nostalgic conservatism encouraged by the return to the Middle Ages, where one was expected to 'revert to the proper channels,/Workings in tapestry, paintings on panels,/And gather up woodcraft's various ambitions' ('The Flight of the Duchess (1845), 232–4). By looking, instead, at the Italian Renaissance, he was following a trend set by popular writers on Renaissance art, which was of special interest to middle-class tourists doing the rounds of Florence, Pisa, Rome and Venice. Ruskin's and Pater's writings form the most erudite outgrowth of this fascination with the art of early modern Italy. For Browning, the increasingly renowned paintings and sculpture of the quattro-cento and cinquecento had much to yield for British culture in the 1840s through to the 1860s, in ways very different from those perceived by Ruskin and Pater. Ruskin, for example, saw in Venetian painting and architecture unbearable manifestations of cultural pride that ultimately corrupted and destroyed the High Renaissance. These were deviations, Ruskin argued, from medieval purity. Pater, by contrast, found his spiritual home among the works of Raphael, Leonardo and Michael-angelo; in fact, he transformed the vices Ruskin identified in the High Renaissance into pre-eminent virtues. Browning showed neither aversion nor commitment to these grand masters. Rather, he was interested in constraints and freedoms afforded by their age – and he looked at them in the belief that the Victorian period was inhabited by men and women who possessed 'wider' but not necessarily better natures. God's revelation in the past had to be glimpsed so that future ambitions might be realised.

The need to place themselves historically became for the Victorians an urgent concern, as John Stuart Mill's famous essays, published in the *Examiner* in 1833 under the heading 'The Spirit of the Age', were among the first to note:

> The 'Spirit of the Age' is in some measure a novel expression. I do not believe that it is to be met with in any work exceeding fifty years in antiquity. The idea of comparing one's own age with former ages, or with our notion of those which are to come, had occurred to philosophers; but it never before was itself the dominant idea of any age.[7]

Mill's idea of the 'Spirit of the Age', adapted and modified from William Hazlitt's earlier writings, became a widely used tag to speak of the sense of what it meant to exist in history. Other major thinkers devised similar catchphrases. In 'Signs of the Times' (1829), Carlyle spoke despairingly of modern 'materialism', bereft of the spiritual 'dynamism' of former times. Belonging to a younger generation, Arnold, likewise, addressed the 'Zeitgeist' in Literature and Dogma (1873), a work which follows a Victorian trend in scrutinising biblical doctrine from a literary point of view.

Each phrase in context – Mill's, Carlyle's, Arnold's – indicates that the Victorians felt at something of a loss in their modernity, and it was in their time that the sense of being 'modern' was making an impression as never before. Ruskin's Modern Painters, like George Meredith's sonnet sequence, Modern Love (1862), draws attention in its title to the distinct historical phase in which the Victorians found themselves situated. The title of one of Browning's poems, too, brings home the clear sense of what it means to belong to one's own time, and this is 'How It Strikes a Contemporary' (1855). In this poem, the speaker, who declares to be unacquainted with poetry, remarks on the only poet he has known in his life. And what was this poet noted for? 'Scenting the world, looking it full in the face' (11). The poem is set in Renaissance Spain; its topic is the poet as a 'recording chief-inquisitor, / The town's true master if the town but knew!' (40). Like Shelley's 'unacknowledged legislator of the world', this poet is extremely knowledgeable about everyday goings on and yet, of necessity, he stands aloof from them. He knows his contemporaries so well that he is obliged to keep his distance – so much so that the speaker has no idea where the poet lives or anything about the life he leads. There are, at least, two amusing ironies in play here: first, in that the poem frames a person who claims he 'could never write a verse' (114); and second, in that the poet, by virtue of reflecting on society, cannot become a part of it. The idea of the poet, then, is doubly displaced – out of the poem and out of the contemporary world while still, in another sense, being integral to both.

To be a poet as well as a contemporary obviously makes for some interesting tensions in Browning's work, and these are drawn out in most extravagant form in *Sordello*, again about a poet, the troubadour celebrated, among many other historical figures, in Dante's *Divine Comedy*. It is the most formidably difficult Victorian poem. This magnificent work attempts to perform several tasks at once in order to grasp the 'spirit of the age' in relation to the past, on this occasion the Guelf–Ghibelline wars that ravaged thirteenth-century Italy. Full details of the exceptionally entangled plot need not be recounted here. Browning's annotated 1863 edition; the *Handbooks* by Alexandra Orr and William Clyde DeVane; a subsequent edition of 1913; and the copious footnotes to the Oxford *Poetical Works*: between them, these manage to extricate its densely woven threads.[8] What matters in the present discussion of historicism is the peculiar structure of the poem, which modulates with great rapidity (often unannounced) between the present time of composition and the setting into which *Sordello* energetically projects itself. *Sordello* not only moves with terrific speed between different historical moments, it also rapidly chops up its narrative sequence – so that the story of war-torn Italy, riven between despots

(Ghibellines) and democrats (Guelfs), which provides the backdrop to Sordello's love for his lady, Palma, has to be pieced together, bit by bit – and this is a huge imposition on the reader (deliberately so). The poem is fully conscious of the challenge to active interpretation it is making. The nature of that challenge derives from the intricate theory of poetic language it is also constructing, again in piecemeal fashion. In sum, *Sordello* is struggling to put an avant-garde method of historiography into poetic practice, as the startling opening lines to the first book indicate:

> Who will, may hear Sordello's story told:
> His story? Who believes me shall behold
> The man, pursue his fortunes to the end,
> Like me: for as the friendless-people's friend
> Spied from his hill-top once, despite the din
> And dust of multitudes, Pentapolin
> Named o' the Naked Arm, I single out
> Sordello, compassed murkily about
> With ravage of six long sad hundred years.
> Only believe me. Ye believe?
>   Appears
> Verona . . . Never, – I should warn you first, –
> Of my own choice had this, if not the worst
> Yet not the best expedient, served to tell
> A story I could body forth so well
> By making speak, myself kept out of view,
> The very man as he wont to do,
> And leaving you to say the rest for him:
> Since, though I might be proud to see the dim
> Abysmal past divide its hateful surge,
> Letting of all men this one man emerge
> Because it pleased me, yet, that moment past,
> I should delight in watching first to last
> His progress as you watch it, not a whit
> More in the secret than yourselves who sit
> Fresh-chapleted to listen.
>   (I. 1–25)

This is self-consciously quixotic writing, plunging us into the heart of an interpretative conundrum. In *Don Quixote*, the protagonist, accompanied by Sancho Panza, sees a dust storm, and infers that this is a clash between two stampeding armies, one of them led by Pentapolin. Quixote, as ever, is making a grave mistake. For the dust that blows 'murkily about' is stirred up, not by armies, but by sheep. This comic allusion to *Don Quixote*, which Browning puts to serious effect, instantly raises the issue of historical perception. How might we discriminate between a flock of sheep and battling armies when dust clouds could point to either of these things? How may we see through the dust to glimpse the 'dim/Abysmal past', enabling 'one man', Sordello, to 'emerge', and take on a living presence?

Browning devises two answers to these questions. First of all, he requires certain licences from his audience; he needs their cooperative 'will' to comprehend Sordello, and so grasp 'His story' (which is also, punningly, 'history'). Second, acutely aware that he cannot tell Sordello's story as Sordello 'was wont to do', he wishes to create a position from where both the narrator and the audience jointly witness the 'progress' at stake. In other words, although the narrator must inevitably tell the story, he wants to keep himself 'out of view', on the margins of the poem. He wishes to be part of the audience, among 'Friends!' (I. 31, 44, 54, and so on) while realising that being a poet is inevitably a 'friendless' task. Like Quixote, therefore, he is the 'friendless-people's friend'. However, having made his point, he has drawn far more attention to himself, and his paradoxical status, than he might wish. Indeed, the narrator does not vanish from sight but constantly interrupts Sordello's story with digressions about how and why the tale is being told. He equivocates throughout about his competence to relate it, and the contradictory place he occupies within it. Later, he realises that the work he has set himself owes much to Shelley, and, while thanking his muse, he lives in fear of it, since his poetry's 'griding screech' (I. 67) would grate on his precursor's ears. Petitioning his audience, and then Shelley, he discovers that, although he desires to be in their company, he is necessarily alone. These are the restless points of anxiety, the awkward ruses, on which *Sordello* turns.

In the course of this opening passage, the historical setting momentarily comes into view, only to be deferred for over sixty lines:

> Lo, the past is hurled
> In twain: up-thrust, out-staggering on the world,
> Subsiding into shape, a darkness rears
> Its outline, kindles at the core, appears
> Verona.
>
> (I. 73–7)

Like breathing back the fire into cooling embers, a picture of Verona is gradually relumed. Some aspects of the political plotting are gradually sketched in, and then the action shifts to Sordello's birthplace, Goito, near Mantua. The narrative method is designed in such a way as to avoid a simple, linear catalogue of names, places and events. Instead, the poem constantly makes lateral connections between key incidents in Sordello's life and the narrator's interjections. Yet, perhaps contrary to expectations, 'Sordello's story', in the course of being haphazardly 'told', is not one of success, since Sordello, in Browning's remodelling of those Italian chronicles that reveal the life of the troubadour, becomes less and less able as a poet as he grows more deeply embroiled in the tumultuous political situation that keeps the Guelfs and Ghibellines at one another's throats. Poetry and politics, here, as elsewhere in Browning's writing, cannot subsist easily together. In this plot of startling peripeties, Sordello is finally caught in a dilemma. Having discovered that he is the son of Taurello Salinguerra, the chief Ghibelline warrior, he is then offered leadership of their party. As a Guelf, he finds this unacceptable. Since he is a poet, it proves impossible. Sordello immediately expires. So rather than tell the tale of a hero, Browning's narrator shifts and slides across the North Italian landscape to outline a story of failure, and ultimately tragedy. But, as the narrator suggests, this story might have turned out otherwise. Sordello has, for sure, auspicious beginnings as a poet. One of his lays wins a Court of Love at Mantua. In fact, so great and unexpected is his prize winning that his main rival, the distinguished Eglamor, dies of shock at his triumph. Yet, like Johannes Agricola, Sordello develops an altogether trumped up opinion of his capabilities. The narrator warns that Sordello foolishly views himself as a veritable 'Monarch of the World' (II. 355), anticipating that his audience will '"bow/Surely in unexampled worship"' (II. 413–14) to him. It is the duty of the narrator to show why such self-aggrandisement will lead to Sordello's ruin, and how, had Sordello only known, the young troubadour could have intervened in the Guelf–Ghibelline conflict and saved future decades from Ecelin of Romano's tyranny.

There are, then, two sides to *Sordello*: 'His story', and the way 'His story' is being narrated. And the narrative commentary, preoccupied with the problems of story telling, points time and again to Sordello's mistakes of judgement. The narrator, throughout the poem, is obsessed with the problem of poetic authority – a problem, to be sure, that is never far from the chief concerns of Browning's writing. If Sordello wrecks his chances as a poet by blowing his own trumpet so loudly, is not the commentator also in danger of committing the same error? To create a clear distinction between Sordello's misguided ambitions and the aims of the true poet, the narrator offers an alternative model of poetry, which is, necessarily, an account of the rationale underpinning *Sordello* itself. The narrator's favoured poet is called the 'Makers-see', a coining that compounds several meanings – God's (the Maker's) seer; the making-of-seeing; and, as a pun, the 'make-us-see'. This kind of poet is the one Browning always theorised: the gifted individual whose role it is to mediate between infinite and finite realms:

> When at some future no-time a brave band
> Sees, using what it sees, then shake my hand
> In heaven, my brother! Meanwhile where's the hurt
> Of keeping the Makers-see on the alert,
> At whose defection mortals stare aghast
> As though heaven's bounteous windows were slammed fast
> Incontinent? Whereas all you, beneath,
> Should scowl at, bruise their lips and break their teeth
> Who ply the pullies, for neglecting you:
> And therefore have I moulded, made anew
> A Man, and give him to be turned at and tried,
> Be angry with or pleased at. On your side,
> Have ye times, places, actors of your own?
> Try them upon Sordello when full-grown,
> And then – ah then! If Hercules first parched
> His foot in Egypt only to be marched
> A sacrifice for Jove with pomp to suit,
> What chance have I?

> (III. 925–42)

Since these important lines are, typically for *Sordello*, very compacted, they need to be rather baldly paraphrased. The narrator begins by stating that when the Second Coming arrives, God and humanity will meet, face to face. Here we see the millennarianism surrounding the historical vision displayed in Browning's earlier poetry. Later poems would move away from such a definitive view of final revelation – or 'no-time'. Here, however, God's children must rely on poets to ease open, and let forth some light from, the windows of heaven. Readers must actively encourage poets to perform this task. Sordello serves as an example of a writer who should be treated in this manner. The trouble is, Sordello never becomes 'full-grown', since he never enjoys an audience that would make him aware of his function as a mediator of God's light. In other words, the narrator entreats us ('makes-us-see') how and why Sordello is not an adequate 'Makers-see'. Yet this leaves open the question of whether the narrator succeeds precisely where Sordello fails.

This point is noticeable in the final sentence where the narrator compares himself to Hercules in Egypt. It is an ironic analogy, carefully placed to question the narrator's authority. For the narrator is implicitly worried about the hubris emanating from his worldly wise statements about who and who does not qualify as a 'Makers-see'. It would seem that the narrator views himself as a far more competent writer than his ostensible subject, Sordello, and this makes him uncomfortable. What is it that gives this commentator the privilege to do right where Sordello does wrong? It is against this question that he recognises the Herculean task he has set himself. At the same time, he shows that even Hercules failed in Egypt. So, although Sordello does not measure up to a 'Makers-see', neither, in a sense, can the narrator – in so far as the narrator knows the necessary limitations and struggles of poets, and Sordello does not. All in all, within this tangled logic, we might say that Browning's commentator has a complete grasp of what it means to be inadequate as a poet, and, in so doing, sees this ultimately as the greatest distinction a poet may enjoy – since a knowledge of one's finitude as a poet gives a clear measure of the ambitious heights to which one must aspire. And yet to make this clear, Browning has had to write to a poem, *Sordello*, that shows that its failure is an index of poetic success, while its subject, Sordello, experiences poetic success as an inevitable form of failure. *Sordello* – a self-confessingly faulted, awkward, jumbled poem – is the work of a 'Makers-see', while Sordello's lays – lyrical, expressive, immediately favoured by a passive public – cannot 'make' their author into a 'seer'.

Sordello's fortunes worsen, in large part, because he misunderstands the function of language. His greatest mistake is to assume an exact correspondence between signs and meanings.

The more he tries to forge the two together, the more his language resists him:

> Piece after piece that armour [his language] broke away,
> Because perceptions whole, like that he sought
> To clothe, reject so pure a work of thought
> As language: thought may take perception's place
> But hardly co-exist in any case,
> Being its mere presentment – of the whole
> By parts, the simultaneous and the sole
> By the successive and the many.
>
> (II. 588–95)

Browning's model of language, and Sordello's confused inversion of it, deserves some explanation, since the terms Browning uses are specific to the poem, rather than Victorian language study in general. There is an internal systematicity to the ideas laid out here. Seeking to contain 'whole' perceptions, essential truths, in language, Sordello presumes that 'thought' (prior to, and productive of, language) actually exists alongside 'perception'. Here, 'thought' might be read as conscious thought or ratiocination. Perception is sensory, concerning the feeling of truth within men and women, and which poetry should bring into consciousness. 'Thought' produces language, and language 'clothes' perception. As a middle term, 'language' rests between 'thought' and 'perception'. 'Thought' replaces 'perception' but cannot be what it replaces. 'Perception', as a truth, cannot be the representation, or 'presentment', which is the domain of language itself – for 'perception' inevitably must be represented in language. To extend this, as the sentence extends, language sunders whole perceptions because it is made up of 'parts' which are 'successive'. In other words, linguistic temporality is forever at odds with perceptual simultaneity. And this is an observation that has considerable implications for the understanding of history.

Relations between the 'simultaneous and the sole' and 'the successive and the many', outlined in this passage, are necessarily impossible ones, because they are based on a fundamental incommensuration. The terms used to define this opposition are especially important because they coincide with key paragraphs in the first of Thomas Carlyle's two essays 'On History' (1830). Browning inventively borrowed Carlyle's theorisation of the 'simultaneous' and the 'successive'. It needs to be borne in mind that Carlyle, an agnostic, anarchic, Tory radical, noted for his truculent writing, held political views remote from Browning's. And his historical projects – such as *Past and Present* (1843), romanticising the pre-capitalist organicism of medieval life, and the life of *Frederick the Great* (1858), monumentalising his doctrine of hero worship – were far from Browning's concerns. But, importantly for Browning, Carlyle was in the grip of the general Victorian questioning of history, and 'On History' stresses, as does *Sordello*, that the past is cannot be accounted for by any one narrative alone. And that is exactly because of the vicissitudes of narrative itself. This is how Carlyle puts his case:

> The most gifted man can observe, still more can record, only the *series* of his own impressions: his observation, therefore, to say nothing of its other imperfections, must be *successive*, while the things done were often *simultaneous*; the things done were not a series, but a group. It is not in acted, as it is in written History: actual events are nowise so simply related to each other as parent and offspring are; every single event is the offspring not of one, but of all other events, prior or contemporaneous, and will in its turn combine with all others to give birth to new: it is an ever-living, ever-working Chaos of Being, wherein shape after shape bodies itself forth from innumerable elements. And this Chaos, boundless as the habitation and duration of man, unfathomable as the soul and destiny of man, is what the historian will depict, and scentifically gauge, we may say, by threading it with single lines of a few ells in length! For as all Action is, by its nature, to be figured

as extended in breadth and in depth, as well as in length; that is to say, is based on Passion and Mystery, if we investigate its origin; and spread abroad on all hands, modifying and modified; as well as advances towards completion, – so all Narrative is, by its nature, of only one dimension; only travels forward towards one, or towards successive points: Narrative is *linear*, Action is *solid*.[9]

Since it is designed to contest the linear compulsions of narrative, *Sordello* creates an illusion of those random groupings that Carlyle claims to be the stuff and substance of history. Carlyle believes that history is distinctly human, and the understanding of it depends on contingent impressions. Such impressions necessarily lead to selective narratives. History writing, therefore, is a subjective affair. And so history – that 'Chaos of Being' – once it is appreciated as an 'ever-living' organic thing, demands that we look at its human characteristics. Carlyle's history writing focuses on the heroics of the past, and how the past was shaped by powerful personalities. For him, history comes alive through the analysis, not of ideological forces (as in Marx), but of great men.

Browning followed Carlyle's theoretical lead, to problematise as well as humanise history, but he was altogether more agonised by the mismatch between historical and perceptual 'simultaneity' and historiographical and linguistic 'successiveness'. The same goes for Browning's treatment of historical subjects. Where Carlyle looks to great prophets of old Browning turns his gaze to altogether lesser figures. This is not to do with a lack of confidence. So prevalent, one might say strenuous, is this interest in the minor and the second rate that it becomes a major component of his aesthetics. For Browning, unlike Carlyle, will not idealise or heroise history. It does not contain for him icons to which we must return – like the benign leadership to be admired, for example, in Abbot Samson of *Past and Present*. He also differed, as Mary Ellis Gibson has remarked, from 'Ruskin and Arnold in representing a historical or aesthetic ideal as a measure of his own culture's deficiencies'. And she adds:

> He too challenged his readers and criticized their culture, but largely by indirection, by presenting them with a new and unmusical poetic language and with a succession of historical characters who are, for the most part, criminals, failures, or dim precursors of some future knowledge or achievement. So Browning chose Sordello not Dante, Andrea del Sarto not Raphael, Karshish not Lazarus, Cleon not Paul, and he embedded his more exemplary historical figures, the Pope and Euripides, in a sordid murder story.[10]

For Browning, it is the minor figure, the one who lives in the shadows of the better known hero, who best embodies history. Sordello, who fails as poet and politician, anticipates the success of Dante as both. This is not in any way concerned with some sentimental love of the underdog or, indeed, the idea that history injudiciously spreads its favours among the undeserving few. Far from it. Nearly all Browning's historical subjects are strategically placed in a significant cultural moment, and they provide a pair of eyes through which that greater figure may be imagined. Yet these minor voices frequently belong to conspicuously limited, some might say disempowered, individuals. Although they offer a perspective on a historical world much larger than themselves, they also allow us to observe that their vision is, for some reason or other, skewed. Often, they are oblivious to things that only we can glimpse with the privilege of hindsight. Sometimes, as with the Duke of Ferrara, their speeches leak meanings that only we, not they, can detect. This point about their imprisoning articulations (they are entrapped in their poems) and our freed interpretations (we can see what they are unable to) has been raised by Carol T. Christ: 'Browning tends not to give his characters historical self-consciousness (with the exception of the pope in *The Ring and the Book*). Like Cleon or Karshish, they inhabit moments they do not understand. Their historical location imposes a blindness upon them which keeps them from understanding the movement of history.'[11] It is their blindnesses that frequently mark out our points of insight. Once more Browning enables his audience to become aware of an ironic differentiation, this time between the speaker's and our own understanding of history.

In turning his gaze to the Italian Renaissance, Browning was concerned not with a longing nostalgia for this time of former artistic glory but with the significance of what was a transitional moment. His major painter poems – 'Pictor Ignotus' (1845), 'Fra Lippo Lippi' (1855) and 'Andrea del Sarto' (1855) – probe the changes that characterised the two phases of the Renaissance, from the advances of the quattrocento (made, for example, by Masaccio and Lippo) to the 'Golden Age' painters (notably, Raphael, Leonardo and Michelangelo). Use of clear-cut linear perspective; development of easel painting; movement towards naturalistic or Mannerist forms: these were altogether new techniques that contributed to the decisive break with the medieval period, and these innovations underlie the conceptual framework of Browning's painter poems.

Furthermore, it was during the Renaissance that the artist became an *individual*. Nineteenth-century European painters celebrated this idea, since, as Leonée Ormond observes, paintings of incidents from the lives of the grand masters proved very popular between 1830 and 1860.[12] Browning did much the same, realising the dramatic potential in Georgio Vasari's *Lives of the Artists* (1550). Yet these painter poems do not concentrate solely on personalities. Each one is preoccupied with the market forces attending the production of such fine works of art. In the fifteenth century mercantile purchases began to count as much as ecclesiastical and ducal patronage, and artists had to comply with the strictures laid down by contractual agreements. Portraits of the Virgin, for instance, were sometimes paid for in square measurements. Pigments, like-wise, were priced according to the value of the precious materials they used. Art was most certainly a business. In this transforming economy, the ironies that give shape and move-ment to Browning's monologues take on cavernous proportions as we come to see how the working and personal lives of the artists stand in stark contrast to the sacred nature of their subjects.

In the course of inventing various psychologies for these acclaimed artists, Browning researched the Renaissance quite thoroughly, but not impeccably. At times, his sources led him astray – as the most learned of his contemporaries noted. But modern criticism of the painter poems can become so bogged down in the identification and attribution of source materials that the central arguments of these poems may almost vanish from sight. It is easy to be misled by a remark made by Dante Gabriel Rossetti (one of Browning's most attentive readers) in 1856: 'I spent some most delightful time with Browning at Paris, both in the evening and at the Louvre, where (and throughout conversation) I found his knowlege of early Italian art beyond that of any one I ever met, – encyclopaedically beyond that of Ruskin himself.'[13] Browning was, indeed, acquainted with all the main authorities – Vasari (his main guide), Filippo Baldinucci (with whom he often disagreed) and Alexis François Rio (who influenced Ruskin and many of Browning's contemporaries). And on the basis of these writ-ings, he was in a position to question some of the suppositions made by his close acquaintance, Anna Jameson, author of two volumes of *Memoirs of the Early Italian Painters and the Progress of Painting in Italy* (1845).[14]

No doubt he felt the High Renaissance had been erroneously idolised, both in its own and Victorian times. Browning's painter poems hardly set it on a pedestal. Rather, he treats the period to forms of light and dark comedy. One poem from *Men and Women*, more lyrical than dramatic, complements those which use an artist as a speaker, and this is 'Old Pictures in Florence'. Exuberant, as well as erudite, this piece of work is generously littered with references to nearly each and every early master. Among the innumerable names are ones which Browning proudly thought he had purchased pictures by. The poem lays out, perhaps more explicitly than anywhere else in Browning's writing, his apprehension of the history of art forms – from those of the ancient world through the Renaissance to the Victorian present. The somewhat jocular tone and incidental use of mischievous rhyme ('Ghirlandajo' (182) and 'heigh ho!' (184), for example) counterpoint the serious contemplation of 'God's clear plan' (112) – which involves the changing modalities of art from one age to another. The poem argues for a dialectical consideration of how and why Greek sculpture and Renaissance painting varied in technique and ambition, and why, moreover, successive generations are driven to aim higher and higher in the pursuit of perfection. Casting his eye on many a mouldering fresco, which the inhabitants of Florence seem hardly worried about, and taking as a chief example Giotto's campanile, which had not by 1853 received the spire that should have originally been placed on top of it, Browning's speaker discusses the plight of himself and his contemporaries as they look to the splendours of the Renaissance, muse upon the ravages of time, and wonder, ultimately, whether nineteenth-century art should bother to emulate the grand designs of their forebears. Art flourishes, it seems, out of this despondent moment:

> Growth came when, looking your last on them all,
>   You turned your eyes inwardly one fine day
> And cried with a start – What if we so small
>   Be greater and grander the while than they?
> Are they perfect of lineament, perfect of stature?
>   In both, of such lower types are we
> Precisely because of our wider nature;
>   For time, theirs – ours, for eternity.

To-day's brief passion limits their range;
　　It seethes with the morrow for us and more.
They are perfect – how else? they shall never change:
　　We are faulty – why not? we have time in store.
The Artificer's hand is not arrested
　　With us; we are rough-hewn, nowise polished:
They stand for our copy, and, once invested
　　With all they can teach, we shall see them abolished.
　　　　　　　　　　　　　　　　　　　　　(113–28)

The accomplishments of the quattrocento serve as a sharp reminder of the artistic inertia of the present, which must, once recognised, be spurred into action. That is, the sublime achievements of former sculptors and painters serve as models for successive generations to create better and even more beautiful art. He is trying to explain how and why each generation senses its obligation to rise above its age, improve it, and perfect it. For Browning believes, in a pervasively Victorian way, that every era in turn impresses its distinctive mark of *progress* on what has gone before. He is unusual, however, in stating that the impulse to create originates in a feeling of cultural impoverishment. Art, for him, is produced within a curious *negativity*. It emerges from those who look to history and discover their 'lower' status, or deficiency, by comparison with past perfection (Greek sculptures; Michaelangelo's murals; and so on). But it progresses because this sense of inadequacy belongs to those who possess, by virtue of historical development, 'wider' natures.

Various metaphors extrapolate this dialectical way of thinking. Like a block of marble, waiting to be modelled, the youngest generation learns the lessons of earlier art practices so as to supersede them and take even more beautiful form. And with time, perhaps, the spire to Giotto's campanile in Florence will be built. It is a model of former architectural – and, by extension, political – ambition waiting for future completion. This is the final note struck by Browning, who looks to Mazzini's heroic efforts to create a unified Italy. Such a future world is altogether preferable to a society governed by a 'monarchy' which 'ever its uncouth cub licks/Out of the bear's shape into the Chimaera's' (270–1). For the liberal-minded Browning, monarchy always threatens to turn into a fire breathing monster. Mazzini's politics, by contrast, promise democratic freedoms: 'Pure Art's birth is still the republic's' (272). And Browning's speaker, ever anticipatory, with a keen and clear eye to the future, declares he is the 'first' (288) to 'foresee' (287) how republicanism, upheld by the motto 'God and the People' (285), will take Italy forward into its own nineteenth-century renaissance, with Giotto's bell tower finally realised as a splendid symbol of cultural renewal.

Previous art, therefore, needs to be understood so that it may be added to, improved and even – and the word emphasises the extremity of the desire here – 'abolished'. This insistence on innovation, observing and then breaking from the past, or drawing from and extending past ambitions, drives at the centre of 'Pictor Ignotus'. The title adopts the phrase used in exhibition catalogues where it has proved impossible to attribute an artist for the illustration in question. There is a slight ambiguity here. 'Ignotus' may mean 'unknown'; it may also imply 'unnoticed'. Browning takes up this commonplace usage to provide some rationale for why certain painters passed unrecognised. Rather than suggest this is a matter of unjust neglect, he indicates that this was in fact a matter of choice. For the pictor who speaks here has had to reach a decision – either to sell his work on the market or to remain in the claustral confines of the church painting a 'monotonous . . . series' of 'Virgin, Babe and Saint,/With the same cold calm beautiful regard' (58, 60–1). He selects the latter. But why? The reasons remain not at all clear without some knowledge of Browning's sources. And, even then, the question of which sources are appropriate to understanding the poem has been a subject of controversy for some time.

Let us begin with the narrative which the poem sketches in. In the opening lines, the painter rather grandly declares that his own skills are comparable to the 'youth's/Ye praise so' (1–2). By the 'youth', he is referring to the highly praised pupils of the quattrocento masters, coming into their own between roughly 1490 and 1520. These younger men would outstrip their teachers in terms of fame. Later, he insists on his insuperable abilities to reproduce the human form in paint: 'all I saw,/Over the canvas could my hand have flung,/Each face obedient to its passion's law' (13–15). Such is his 'gift/Of fires from God' (5–6). These claims are made with considerable ease. The verb 'flung', for instance, has an air of casual grace, yet, when prefaced with the conditional tense ('could have'), there is some possibility that his technique is not all that he makes it out to be. However, the tone, even if its sincerity is questionable, is self-assured. The first forty lines comprise two flourishing sentences. The extended syntax complements the painter's self-esteem. His vocabulary, similarly, is full of verbs connected with growth and development: 'springs up' (2), 'outburst' (4), 'uplift' (7), and so on. Aspiration is all. Yet we realise, at the same time, that he is talking about his own past – for the pictures personifying 'Hope' (17), 'Rapture' (19), and 'Confidence' (21), about which he speaks so enthusiastically, and indeed brings to life as he remembers them, are no more. Such things have not been 'saved' (24). What remains is a dream of success that never was. He is left with a fantasy of what he might have achieved – favours at court, public demonstrations celebrating his fame, universal renown.

Something stopped him. Exactly what remains unclear. The painter says that 'a voice changed' (41) his plans. But the identity of this 'voice' is vague. Whether it was the voice of conscience, of God, or of some other authority, it none the less dictated his fate to him. That said, it is obvious that the open market offends him. He cannot stand the idea of prostituting his works to customers, who, in his opinion, vulgarly treat art like 'garniture and household-stuff' (51). And he seems proud that 'no merchant traffics in' his 'heart' (62). Yet this is his only recompense for the fame he has not realised. And so, in the depths of the crypt, he works busily on wet plaster – watching his paintings, amid the dampness, fade, peel, flake and, inevitably, 'die' (69).

What might we infer from the pictor's story? To begin with, it is possible to read the poem as Browning's reaction to the precepts of Romanticism. The painter's dream of personal glory extends into an idealised marriage of art and artist: 'I and my picture, linked/With love about, and praise, till life should end, /And then not go to heaven' (36–8). Such words suggest that the Romantic impulse to coalesce subject and object – making artist, art work, and the world at large one and the same thing – is to try to create a heaven on earth, and that this is a fallacy. Perhaps that is why the painter now faces a dismal prospect. His predicament leads to several other questions.

Has the painter done the right thing by turning his back on the commercial world, reconciling himself to an art that can only 'die'? Is this inward looking cloistered darkness somehow a purer place for art? Or should he have embraced the market to fulfil his glorious ambitions? Or would that have been despicably self-seeking? He is in an awkward situation, since it would seem that both the market and the crypt, in different ways, degrade art. The artist is caught between competing demands – to the people and to God. And we may choose to think that he plays safe by consigning himself to the darkness of obscurity where he can let his fantasies run free. But, to make a final point here, the market, whether he likes it or not, has caught up with him – for the works of 'pictor ignotus' are now, in the mid-nineteenth century, appearing before the public eye. And, what is more, he is embodied, individualised, in Browning's poem.

Audiences always preyed on Browning's mind, and in 'Pictor Ignotus' we can see how that anxiety is being worked through, remaining, in the end, unresolved. None the less, scholars as interested as Browning was in Italian art have reached more decisive conclusions about why the painter elected to stay within the confines of the church. These arguments can be illuminating. For this cinquecento artist (the poem is subtitled 'Florence 15 –'), envious of 'that youth', seems to have turned his back, for some reason or other, on the fashions of his day. As Victorian writers on the Italian Renaissance have often noted, there was a distinctive break between the spiritually orientated work of the early quattrocento and the much more humanised, some might say 'pagan', art that followed Raphael. J. B. Bullen has suggested – to much protest – that Browning's 'Pictor Ignotus' draws on, and remodels, Vasari's life of Fra Bartolommeo, and identifies the 'voice' of line 41 as that of Savonarola, the priest who forged a movement against the increasingly sensual art he believed was disgracing the church.[15] Savonarola organised ritual burnings of paintings he deemed sacrilegious – the so-called bonfires of the vanities. He was furious at the new 'pagan' art (later favoured by Vasari, and which, in Browning's own time, troubled Ruskin and many other Victorians). Bartolommeo, formerly known as Baccio della Porta, renounced his early work, became one of Savonarola's disciples, and was besieged with his leader in San Marco when events turned against such religious fanaticism. He then joined the Dominicans, gave up painting for a while, and later came into contact with the younger Raphael, who admired and taught 'Il Frate' the art of perspective.

Bullen's most convincing point concerns the ambivalence Vasari felt towards those artists, like Bartolommeo, whose work evinced greatness in the face of their regressive sectarian interests, since Vasari generally believed that the naturalistic paintings of the High Renaissance were far richer than their predecessors. Vasari was Browning's main source in 1845, and it seems in 'Pictor Ignotus' there is some agreement that where the 'youth's' naturalistic style wins fame, the older form of religious art, in all its introspection, must 'die'. Yet this does not necessarily mean that Browning's poem is arguing in favour of commercialism, and all that goes along with it. Nor should it imply that Vasari's life of 'Il Frate' is the indisputably correct source. In any case, the poem seems to draw on an incident noted in Vasari's life of Cimabue, as Ormond has shown.[16] Rather Bullen's hypothesis usefully indicates how Browning's painter poems are entangled in the complex Victorian debates about the relative values of early and late (spiritual and pagan) quattrocento painting. 'Fra Lippo Lippi', published ten years later, explores this difference of styles from a rather different angle, and with a number of other authorities, not just Vasari, in mind.

In her popular guide to Italian painting, Anna Jameson had this to say about Fra Lippo Lippi:

This libertine monk was undoubtedly a man of extraordinary genius, but his talent was degraded by his immorality: he adopted and carried on all the improvements of Masaccio, and was the first who invented that particular style of grandeur and breadth in the drawing of his figures, the grouping, and the contrast of light and shade, and afterwards carried to such perfection by Andrea del Sarto. He was one of the earliest painters who introduced landscape background, painted with some feeling for the truth of nature; but the expression he gave to his personages, though always energetic, was often inappropriate, and never calm or elevated: in the representation of sacred incidents he was sometimes fantastic and sometimes vulgar; and he was the first who desecrated such subjects by introducing the portraits of women who happened to be the objects of his preference at the moment.[17]

Jameson's somewhat prescriptive judgements largely relied on an influential work by Rio – *The Poetry of Christian Art*, published in Paris in 1836, and translated into English in 1854.

Rio advanced the view that early quattrocento art was 'Idealist', spiritually pure and noble, unlike that of the later 'Naturalist' school, which <u>de</u>meaningly used mistresses as Madonnas, as did Fra Lippo Lippi. Certainly, there was much in Lippo's life that would offend prurient Victorians. He anticipated, perhaps more than any other artist, the triumphs the High Renaissance. As Jameson says, Lippo was noted for his use of 'relievo', a system of lighting and shading which Mannerist painters, such as Andrea, exploited to give greater roundness, height and depth to their figures.

A. Dwight Culler sees Browning's poem as a 'direct reply to Mrs Jameson', refuting her moral condemnation of the artist.[18] But this reply was not simply a counter-argument. Culler observes Browning's complicated reshuffling of source material at work within the poem, suggesting that remarks by Jameson about Masaccio – 'it was said of him that he painted souls as well as bodies'[19] – were mapped on to the biography of Fra Lippo Lippi because the brother's life contained episodes which availed themselves to an altogether more engaging type of drama: 'Browning wanted Fra Lippo's career to have not merely individual significance but to be representative of a new movement in art history. There was nothing in Masaccio's life that would dramatize that change, and therefore the change was associated with Fra Lippo'.[20] Elements of Vasari's life of Lippo are, of course, kept intact in the poem.

The main point is that Browning was using a very free hand with his sources. For what concerned him most was finding a suitable dramatic vehicle to mediate his views on art. And Jameson's writing was clearly an incentive to make his position clear on the relative merits of early and late quattrocento styles. In 'Fra Lippo Lippi' he seems to want to break down the division that Rio, Jameson, and several other commentators had placed between them. Browning wished to bring 'souls' and 'bodies' – divine wisdom and sexual creativity – into a positive conjunction. His was a characteristically liberal and open-minded response. Yet it involved a remarkable balancing act. As David J. DeLaura remarks: '"Fra Lippo Lippi" is an important document in the mid-century attempt to reconcile soul and flesh, old idealism and new naturalism, without quite giving up the traditional theological framework.'[21]

Examining the context of Browning's painter poems, De-Laura shows just how complexly 'Fra Lippo Lippi' is caught up in ideological fields where the opposing forces of religion and sexuality are entangled in a network of Roman Catholic and Protestant prejudices ignited during the 1850s. Rio's Catholicism encouraged him to favour the non-realist spiritual endeavours of the early painters. Jameson, meanwhile, agreed, but, as a Protestant, she was obliged to couch her argument in terms that ensured she did not appear a Catholic sympathiser. She was writing at a time when the Catholic hierarchy was being reestablished in Britain, to much controversy. Against Rio, other Protestants, such as Charles Kingsley, complained about the 'effeminacy' cultivated by such Catholic tastes. Here Browning followed suit, for Fra Lippo Lippi is forever breaking his vow of celibacy. DeLaura notes the 'vitality' that emerges from the 'utter implausibility of making a scampish and illiterate fifteenth-century Italian monk the mouthpiece of the new Protestant realism in art'.[22] Browning, then, is using the voice of one who constantly wandered out of the cloister in search of sex (and who, despite that, remained a great artist) to overturn Rio's preference for an ascetic art that was closer to the medieval period than the provocative eroticism of the High Renaissance. Browning's Protestantism was far from self-abnegating – it belonged to a strain of middle-class radicalism that saw sexual love as God's gift, not sin.

Lippo's sexual transgressions are noted in the very first lines of Browning's poem. He has been caught by the watch in a backstreet where 'sportive ladies' (6) ply their trade, and it is probable that the guards are threatening to arrest him on suspicion of entering a brothel. His speech is given over to

placating the guards who could all too easily turn him over to
the authorities. He argues garrulously – about his reasons for
being out at night, his childhood and his views on art. Unlike
pictor ignotus, Lippo does not enjoy being imprisoned in his
'mew' for three weeks 'A-painting . . . saints and saints, / And
saints again' (46–9) – his current commission for Cosimo di
Medici. Instead, his 'flesh and blood' (60) urge him out of
doors. He protests he did not choose a monastic life. A beggar
until the age of eight, he was discovered by the vigilant Prior to
have a talent for drawing – and so he found himself, with food
and shelter, among the Carmelites where he had relative
freedom to practise his skills.

The trouble is, in later life he produced art that was far
too realistic for the Prior's liking, since it revealed Lippo's
restive sexuality. As Lippo insists: 'You should not take a fellow
eight years old / And make him swear to never kiss the girls'
(224–5). His fellow monks observed that one of the women he
depicted was '"like the Prior's niece who comes / To care
about his asthma"' (170–1). The Prior, echoing Anna Jameson, would prefer pictures in the style of Giotto whose '"Saint
a-praising God, / . . . sets us praising"' (189–90). The Prior
also glimpses the presence of his 'niece' (mistress, daughter, or
both?) in one of Lippo's pictures, this time as Herodias, the
sensual wife of Herod, who plotted with Salome to behead
St John. Lippo, no doubt, was enjoying an affair with her.
Criticism of Lippo's fleshly style remains unabated:

> the old grave eyes
> Are peeping o'er my shoulder as I work,
> The heads shake still – 'It's art's decline, my son!
> You're not of the true painters, great and old;
> Brother Angelico's the man, you'll find;
> Brother Lorenzo stands his single peer:
> Fag on at flesh, you'll never make the third!'
>
> (231–7)

(Jameson praised the spiritually pure art of Fra Angelico, Lippo's contemporary, highly: 'To Angelico the art of painting a picture devoted to religious purposes was an act of religion, for which he prepared himself by fasting and prayer'.)[23]

Facing these charges, Lippo vigorously defends himself. An innovator, he knows exactly what he is aiming for, taking the human figure to 'Make his flesh liker and his soul more like' (207). And his ambitions rest on a biblical paradigm from Genesis:

> I think I speak as I was taught;
> I always see the garden and God there
> A-making man's wife: and, my lesson learned,
> The value and significance of flesh,
> I can't unlearn ten minutes afterwards.
> (265–9)

In Eden, under God's eye, Adam and Eve combined their bodies and their souls. In this scene before the Fall, sexual love bore no shame. Lippo's art adheres to this model. And, more than that, he believes that this approach to art is a good augury for the future. 'I know what's sure to follow' (280), he says. He mentions his promising pupil, 'Hulking Tom': Tommaso Masaccio. (Masaccio means 'hulking', 'sloppy', or 'clumsy'.) Yet, as Jameson states in her *Memoirs*, Lippo extended the *older* Masaccio's style. Why did Browning make Lippo the originator of the new 'pagan' sensuality? Was he simply misled by a footnote in the Milanesi edition of Vasari's *Lives* on which he relied?[24] After more research, he was not perturbed when he discovered that Vasari's *Life* was, as he said in 1866, a 'tissue of errors'.[25] Browning was not finical about what he considered a minor mistake.

For it is the irrepressible energy of Lippo that lies at the centre of the poem, and so grabs our attention more than anything else. And he gives of himself generously, both in his

speech and his art: his huge spectacular pictures overwhelm
their spectators with life giving realism. He is indefatigably
responsive to the day to day 'business of the world' (247). His
each and every sense is fully orchestrated here. Tastes and
smells prompt some remarkable similes: 'the air this spicy night
. . . turns/the unaccustomed head like Chianti wine!' (339).
He interlards snippets of song (based on the Tuscan *stornelli*)
into his speech, and these burst in upon his way of talking to
suggest he is more naturally a singer than a talker. His song
celebrates the symbolism of flowers: the peach, the clove, the
pine, and so on, and these have sexual connotations. The
natural world for him 'means intensely, and means good:/To
find its meaning is my meat and drink' (314–15). All of it
abounds in sensuous pleasures: he revels in its 'beauty and the
wonder and the power,/The shapes of things, their colours,
lights and shades' (283–4). His 'cup runs over' (250), while
that of pictor ignotus, by contrast, has been 'spilt' (23). A
traitor to his faith, Lippo works exceedingly hard at his com-
missions – even if he has to 'swallow' his 'rage' (243) at his
patrons' whims. A good Protestant before his time, he gets on
with the tasks set before him.

There is much to forgive this provocative and life loving
rogue, particularly when he is so honest about his ambitious
commitment to producing better and stronger works of art.
Towards the close of his monologue he elaborates his plans for
a painting he shall complete within the next six months. His
most realistic work of art will be the one in which he finds room
for a portrait of himself:

> I shall paint
> God in the midst, Madonna and her babe,
> Ringed by a bowery flowery angle-brood,
> Lilies and vestments and white faces, sweet
> As puff on puff of grated orris-root
> When ladies crowd to Church at midsummer . . .

> Well, all these
> Secured at their devotion, up shall come
> Out of a corner when you least expect,
> As one by a dark stair into a great light,
> Music and talking, who but Lippo! I! –
> Mazed, motionless and moonstruck – I'm the man!
>
> (347–52, 359–64)

Browning probably had in mind here Lippo's *The Coronation of the Virgin*, in which the artist was at one time believed to have portrayed himself as the figure carrying a staff in the far right of the painting. (Subsequent scholarship has shown this not to be the case.)[26] What might we make of Lippo's surprise entrance into his most ambitious work? As Lippo says, his appearance among 'this presence, this pure company' (368) of saints and angels causes him some embarrassment, for perhaps two reasons. First, he is not exactly 'pure'; and second, there is a discomfiting pride in placing oneself at the centre of one's art. But some 'sweet angelic slip of a thing' (370) – one of his female admirers, whom he has depicted as a divine spirit – assures him that such self-portraiture is justified, since he should be recognised for what he is: a great painter, loved by young women, some of whom had kindly spoken 'a good word for' him 'in the nick' of time (386). On various occasions, they have saved him from charges of adultery. And so, with a 'blushing face' (378), he decides to do what he always does when some 'hothead husband' (383) threatens to catch him in the arms of a pretty young wife – he makes a quick escape to 'some safe bench behind' (384), still holding firm the hand of his paramour. So his ambiguous position in his painting sums up his role in life: he waits in the margins, officially forbidden to participate in the sexual world around him, but none the less making an unofficial entry into it.

Lippo's ambivalent act of self-portraiture perhaps reveals an indecisiveness on Browning's part about the cultural function and location of the mid-Victorian artist. This is certainly not stretching a point, given the intense discussions of spiritual and secular styles in the Renaissance provoked by Ruskin, Rio and Jameson, along with the Roman Catholic resurgence of the early 1850s. Furthermore, the activities of the Pre-Raphaelite brotherhood stirred up considerable controversy by returning to what were considered to be first principles in an attempt to recover forgotten techniques in colour and line. They, too, were investigating the break between early and late phases of Renaissance painting, creating their own distinctive aesthetics, very different from Browning's.

How might these differing invocations of the Italian Renaissance speak on behalf of Victorian perceptions of what it meant to be an artist? It could be said that in 'Fra Lippo Lippi' Browning was negotiating the idea of where the artist might stand in relation to his work – inside it, outside it or somewhere in between. For where might Browning be placed here? As a voice haunting Lippo's? As a name we take on trust as having created the poem yet whose presence can only be imagined as its frame? One problem with the use of the dramatic persona was the potential disappearance of the author altogether. Given, on the one hand, Browning's devotion to the lives of artists (biographies which could stand as devices to interpret works of art) and, on the other, his belief that the poet was instrumental in mediating divine truth to humanity (like the 'Makers-see'), he was working with a form that threatened to belie his ostensible aims. By rewriting the lives of the artists, Browning had, problematically, written himself out. Possibly Lippo's marginal self-portrait signals Browning's fear of self-erasure?

'Andrea del Sarto' filters Browning's views on artistic practice by focusing on several notorious incidents from the life of a cinquecento painter renowned for his 'faultless' technique. Where Lippo turns his attention to ever more ambitious projects, Andrea suffers from a dwindling resource of energy.

Their respective art works belong to different phases of the Renaissance and their lives are at entirely opposite poles. Lippo is a healthy libertine; Andrea is tiringly respectable. Like his contemporary, pictor ignotus, Andrea measures himself against the achievements of Raphael – who marked for the Victorians the crucial break between quattrocento and High Renaissance styles. But Andrea sees himself, not so much as Raphael's rival, but his better. Eyeing a figure in one of Raphael's 'flaming' (186) frescos on a Roman 'palace-wall' (187), he claims that 'indeed the arm is wrong' (194), and that he alone could correct it. Michaelangelo has said as much to Andrea himself. So what is preventing Andrea, a greatly talented painter from achieving the kind of fame enjoyed by Raphael? Passages from the scandalous first edition of Vasari's *Lives* reveal that Andrea's disappointments lay in his obsessive desire for a young woman who would become his most prized possession:

> At that time there was a most beautiful girl in the Via di San Gallo, who was married to a capmaker, and, who, though born of a poor and vicious father, carried about her as much pride and haughtiness as beauty and fascination. She delighted in trapping the hearts of men, and among others ensnared the unlucky Andrea, whose immoderate love for her soon caused him to neglect the studies demanded by his art, and in great measure to discontinue the assistance which he had given to his parents.
>
> Now it chanced that a sudden and grievous illness seized the husband of this woman, who rose no more from his bed, but died thereof. Without taking counsel of his friends therefore; without regard to the dignity of his art or the consideration due to his genius, and to the eminence he had attained with so much labour; without a word, in short, to any of his kindred, Andrea took the hand of this Lucrezia di Baccio del Fede, such was the name of the woman, to be his wife; her beauty appearing to him to merit thus much as his hands.[27]

Vasari tells of how Andrea would do anything to please

Lucrezia, so much so that he was willing to relinquish the patronage of King Francis I of France:

> [Having worked for some time for the French king] he received a letter, after having had many others, from Lucrezia his wife, whom he had left disconsolate for his departure, although she wanted for nothing. Andrea had even ordered a house to be built for them behind the Nunziata, giving her hopes that he might return at any moment; yet as she could not give money to her kindred and connexions, as she had previously done, she wrote with bitter complaint to Andrea, declaring that she never ceased to weep, and was in perpetual affliction at his absence; dressing all this up with sweet words, well calculated to move the heart of this luckless man, who loved her but too well, she drove the poor soul half out of his wits; above all, when he read her assurance that if he did not return to her speedily, he would certainly find her dead. Moved by all this, he resolved to resume his chain, and preferred a life of wretchedness with her to the ease around him, and to all the glory which his art must have secured to him. He was then too so richly provided with handsome vestments by the liberality of the king and his nobles, and found himself so magnificently arrayed, that every hour seemed a thousand years to him, until he could go to show himself in his bravery to his beautiful wife. Taking the money which was confided to him for the purchase of pictures, statues, and other fine things, he set off therefore, having first sworn on the Gospels to return within a few months. Arrived happily in Florence, he lived joyously with his wife for some time, making large presents to her father and sisters, but doing nothing for his own parents, whom he would not even see, and who at the end of a certain period, ended their lives in great poverty and misery.[28]

It is an intriguing story, laying the blame of one man's artistic failure on both his patron's overgenerosity and his wife's fickle desires. Browning decided to turn this narrative inside out, attributing much greater responsibility to Andrea, rather than Francis I and Lucrezia, for his eventual decline. Unlike Vasari (who had been del Sarto's pupil, and who seemed to hold a personal grudge against Lucrezia), Browning saw the celebrated 'perfection' of Andrea's work as the artist's major weakness. In the poem, the painter's 'faultlessness' becomes the very cause of his inability to succeed. And his speech is given over to a poignant moment late in his career when he has come to recognise how and why he has failed. Yet, in his brief review of the many wrongs he has committed, Andrea cannot change his course, for he interprets his fate as God's inevitable punishment.

The opening lines discover him pleading with Lucrezia to remain by his side a short while longer. They have been quarrelling, and from what we can gather she has been trying to strike some kind of bargain with him. She will stay his pleasure as long as he agrees to paint her picture for her 'friend's friend' (5). He must do this by the time and at the price fixed by that client. This euphemistically named 'friend' is obviously one of Lucrezia's lovers. Andrea, forever obsessed with her beauty, will comply. Yet this is not an entirely one-sided transaction, even if he ultimately loses out. He reminds her that he needs her to sit for 'each of the five pictures we require:/It saves a model' (24–5). She still has to work for him. Lucrezia's demands, however, outstrip what remains of his business sense, for the pictures she passes on to her variously named 'friend' and 'Cousin' (220) act as guarantees against that lover's 'gaming debts' (222).

Now that their argument has ended, Andrea holds Lucrezia's hand, watching the sun set over Fiesole in the autumn – where everything is suggestively 'toned down' (39). He calls the scene before him a 'twilight-piece' (48). Here, amid this 'common greyness' (35), he imagines how they should look as man and wife: her 'soft hand is a woman of itself' and his the 'bared breast she curls inside' (21–2). This is how he would like to be seen. Yet so desiccated is their love, he can only visualise its outline in monochrome. Worse still, he hardly sees Lucrezia as a person at all. She is, for him, simply a captivating face he can copy perfectly: 'You smile? why, there's my picture ready made' (33). By his own design, Lucrezia is his commodity. She is exchanged, by way of art, between her lovers (his customers) and her husband (their employee). And so she remains, in a double sense, 'very dear' (32). He has to bear the great cost of his desire, since his struggles to keep her in his company lead him to sell his work below its market price. She is 'dear' in a way that impoverishes him – both artistically and financially. This marriage has proved a bad deal. But still he clings to a decorously falsifying image of it.

His art has been reified, since it comes too easily for him to put it to any productive use. In no way does Andrea exercise his talents:

> I can do with my pencil what I know,
> What I see, what at bottom of my heart
> I wish for, if I ever wish so deep –
> Do easily, too – when I say, perfectly,
> I do not boast, perhaps: yourself are judge,
> Who listened to the Legate's talk last week,
> And just as much they used to say in France.
>
> (60–6)

Such words are lost on Lucrezia. She does not 'care to understand about' his 'art' (54). 'Carelessly passing' through his studio, her 'robes afloat', she has unthinkingly 'smeared' his canvases (74–5). She would seem to have good reason to do so. For as he tries to reproach her, it becomes patently clear that his failure rests on his inflated pride. Assured of his skills, Andrea remains conceited and self-centred, selfishly 'painting from myself and to myself . . ./unmoved by men's blame/Or their praise either' (90–2). Imagining his whole world in terms of pictures, not persons, he discloses that his faultless art is more precious to him than anything else. It is because of this, as he admits, that his paintings lack 'soul' (108, 113).

Andrea, if a perfect technician, is condemned to remain a 'craftsman' (82), not a true artist. The celebrated triumvirate – Leonardo, Michaelangelo and Raphael – have 'a truer light of God in them' (79) because they aspire, and 'reach a heaven that's shut' (84) to Andrea, for all the inadequacies of their work. In the most quoted line in the poem, he apprehends how 'a man's reach should exceed his grasp' (97). Sadly, he cannot bring himself to put that knowledge into practice. He prefers obscurity – where his arrogant fantasies of artistic and sexual power can run wild. His is a self-imposed exile. He has escaped from the world outside, and the risks it involves. A '"sorry little scrub"' (189), as Michaelangelo calls him, he has long lived in fear of being discovered by the Paris lords who may fetch him back to Francis I. Holed up in his studio, he is left to contemplate his legacy:

> 'Rafael did this, Andrea painted that;
> The Roman's is the better when you pray,
> But still the other's Virgin was his wife –'
> Men will excuse me.
> (177–80)

This idealised picture of marriage is his threadbare compensation for the talents he has squandered. Such illusions of respectability allow him to block out painful truths, in particular the fact that Lucrezia is more of a mistress than a Madonna. One other point needs to be noted here. Andrea, unlike Leonardo and Michaelangelo, was not homosexual. This thought obsesses him to the end: 'the three first without a wife, / While I have mine' (264–5). Yet, in Victorian terms, their far from acceptable desires have led to art altogether greater than Andrea's. Indeed, the love he felt from Francis I would appear to have been more intense and more intimate than any he had known. He fondly refers to 'that humane great monarch's golden look' (153), remembering, in a telling repetition, the appreciative look in the king's 'eyes,/Such frank French eyes' (159–60). In fact, Francis seems to have grown physically closer to Andrea than anyone else in his life – 'One arm about my shoulder, round my neck . . . I painting proudly with his breath on me' (156–8). Perhaps Andrea suggests, in spite of his dreams of marital bliss, that an illicit love between men or at least a form of male homoeroticism – so perverse to the Victorian mind – is in some respect more preferable to him than the atrophied state of marriage in which he now finds himself? Possibly it is reasonable to claim that the poem opens a sado-masochistic structure of desire dividing between the pains he suffers at the hands of Lucrezia – and which he seems to invite – and the joys of Francis' court – which he self-punishingly rejected?[29]

Celebrating the imperfect; taking risks; straying from the norm: these are fundamental transgressions from which the highest creativity springs. But, as Andrea himself acknowledges, 'All is as God over-rules' (134). No matter how venturesome art may be, it is always governed by a divine plan. The lives of Renaissance painters are necessarily subsumed within a larger conception of human history – one which testifies to God's ever unfolding revelation in the world with its changing demands on art and artists. Andrea's historical function is to show how the infinite is manifest when art struggles to surpass its limits. He is in possession of this knowledge but cannot do away with his overweening pride to set his mind to innovate in the manner of his great contemporaries. Instead, he is left contemplating how he would correct his rivals' mistakes.

It might be said that 'Andrea del Sarto' is performing much the same function since it details its subject's errors. Yet these two negativities – the poem's and Andrea's – are not entirely symmetrical. Although Browning's poem points to Andrea's limitations so that its reach may be considered to exceed the painter's grasp, and so may be thought to duplicate Andrea's arrogance towards others, 'Andrea del Sarto' has attempted to do what Andrea has not. And that is to respond to the demands of its age. This was the demand to remake history – to see how past events could be imaginatively remodelled for present uses. But, in this poem, there is a lingering sense that Browning is more of the master of the historical plan God is supposed to have put into action than God himself. Perhaps this is simply a matter of a Victorian's historical advantage?

Just as benighted as Andrea is Cleon, the first-century Greek poet. His fault is his inability to accept Christianity, and forgo the outdated pretensions of his pagan culture. His name entitles the poem of 1855 which accounts for the despairing limits to his vision. For a setting, Browning has, once more, chosen a moment anticipating considerable cultural change – St Paul's missions to Cyprus, Asia Minor and Greece that began in approximately AD 47. This is the only historical inference we can make for certain, and it is the most crucial piece of evidence to hand. Cleon himself has no basis in fact, and the 'tyrant' he works for, Protus, is also imaginary. There is a poem entitled 'Protus' in *Men and Women*, and there Browning lets the name stand for one of the scores of 'Half-emperors and quarter-emperors' (2), almost entirely forgotten now, whose images are to be found among the innumerable busts, sculpted by Greek artists in the service of Rome. This Protus is surrounded by all sorts of amusingly obscure legends – one of which claims he was usurped by a 'blacksmith's bastard' (37), John the Pannonian, and allowed to slip away to 'some blind northern court' (47) where his only achievement was to have written a 'little tract "On worming dogs"' (50). Such is the fate of would be tyrants.

Yet the name Protus (in Latin, 'princeps') was held by all the emperors who reigned after Augustus Caesar. In 'Cleon', given Protus' fondness for Greek culture, it is possible Browning was thinking of Nero, a philhellene, infamous for his persecution of Christians. The parallel is slight but it none the less points to the clash of interests between the Roman enchantment with

109

the prestige attached to things Greek and the subversive force of Christianity, increasingly favoured by the disempowered. It would take three centuries before Emperor Constantine founded St Peter's church in Rome, and by then the Roman Empire was on the brink of collapse. Greek art was by the first century living off past glories, having been subject to Rome for two hundred years by the time Cleon is speaking. Living at the tail end of classical culture, Cleon embodies a sterile form of antiquity. He cannot envisage a productive, life giving future such as the one Paul offers his followers as he spreads God's word among the oppressed.

The poem opens with Cleon's eulogy to his tyrannous patron. Protus has just delivered a gallery richly laden with gifts, and Cleon duly thanks his master for his 'munificence' (19). Expert in 'all arts' (61), Cleon has pleased him by performing a formidable multitude of tasks. He has written epic poetry now inscribed upon plates of gold, composed the lyric chanted by local fishermen, designed an image of Apollo upon a lighthouse, pictured in exact proportions the human anatomy, and completed a philosophical treatise on the soul. He is understandably famed throughout the 'seventeen isles' (63) of Protus' colony where the tyrant has built a tower to 'look out to the East' (35). This remarkable polymath declares that Protus' architectural achievement marks the highest point of culture. Among these 'sprinkled isles' (1), probably the Sporades, the king has created an outpost where he has the best of art and politics. Cleon, admiring the Apollonian ambitions of the tower, views it as a monument to divine aspiration. For Protus surely deserves to have 'some eventual rest a-top of it' (33), reclining among the gods. And yet the tower serves to keep an eye on everything beneath it – slaves; trading vessels; armies; and, of course, Cleon himself.

It is clear to see how Protus' politics are dressed up in his aesthetics. To Cleon, 'black and white slaves' appear 'like the chequer-work/Pavement' (12–13). Another slave, who sweetly sings her master's praises, is referred to as a 'lyric woman' (15); her bright 'crocus vest' (15) has been extravagantly 'Woven of sea-wools' (16). For Cleon, these sensory delights amount to 'joy' (21) – the very highest 'use of life' (22). But as his letter to his patron unfolds, it becomes glaringly apparent that such aspirations and the 'joy' deriving from them are questionable. Certainly, the 'calm' that Protus desires has not been discovered, since it is, in a repeated adjective, 'eventual' (33, 42). And, indeed, Protus turns to Cleon for some answer to his own anxieties at the prospect of death, and the possible withering of his empire. Answering these anxious enquiries, Cleon realises that Protus' work belongs to a historical 'sequence' (74) that is as yet incomplete; Protus' extraordinary achievements are 'to be viewed eventually/As a great whole' (76–7). But how that 'whole' might be conceptualised within a pagan system of belief proves very difficult for Cleon. Lacking Christian knowledge, the Greek artist is faced with a fatally nihilistic outlook – where art, unable to tend towards some higher aim, must contemplate its devastation. The future holds the bleakest of prospects for both patron and client. It threatens to erase them and so render their labours meaningless.

Cleon time and again searches for an answer to the pressing question of historical 'effacement' (80). If each art work from successive ages is 'pronounced complete' (79), it proves difficult for Cleon to grasp how each finished piece, seen as perfect in itself, can form part of a progressive or cumulative view of history. He apprehends how the efforts of each generation contribute to an overall 'synthesis' (94), but he cannot infer what its purpose might be. Since Zeus has provided no clues, Cleon has created his own myth of cultural development. He imagines how Zeus would have revealed the secret, had the god spoken:

> our soul, misknown, cries out to Zeus
> To vindicate his purpose in our life:

Why stay we on the earth unless to grow?
Long since, I imaged, wrote the fiction out,
That he or other god descended here
And, once for all, showed simultaneously
What, in its nature, never can be shown,
Piecemeal or in succession; – showed, I say,
The worth both absolute and relative
Of all his children from the birth of time,
His instruments for all appointed work.
I now go on to image, – might we hear
The judgement which should give due to each,
Show where the labour lay and where the ease,
And prove Zeus' self, the latent everywhere!
This is a dream: –

(112–27)

Since Zeus has provided no answer, Cleon has had to create a fiction for himself to explain this crisis, and this considerable act of imagination has brought him close to the brink of profound understanding. Once more, it is the creative power of poetry that generates the most significant insights available to men and women. But, by virtue of his historical position, Cleon is unable to progress to the critical point of knowledge marked by the advent of Christianity. Like the narrator of *Sordello*, he comprehends that the 'whole' – that is, the meaning and purpose of cultural history – cannot be revealed in nature, since nature is made up of fragmentary parts. As in *Sordello*, the simultaneous and the sole are forever dispersed among the successive and the many. Had Zeus made his 'judgement' known to all those who 'work' and 'labour' in his name, then there would be an ethics on which life could be based. Each person would have his or her 'due'. Work would be justly rewarded.

Here, once again, one of Browning's personae speaks on be-half of a Protestant belief in God as a just task-master, although he remains without the historical privilege to comprehend the full implications of what he is saying. Zeus, of course, does not possess the revelatory power of the Christian God. If anything, Zeus is a violent and unloving deity, one close to the Calvinist idea of a divine being whose punishments are unremitting. A late poem, 'Ixion' (1883), would seem to bear out this point; there Zeus 'Doles out – old yet young – agonies ever afresh' (6). Browning's conception of God is altogether more benevolent, permitting individual freedoms and choices, and then generously acknowledging them. This distinction between strands of Protestantism is important to note since many commentators have sought to consign Browning to a morally stern Evangelicalism, especially on the basis of *Christmas-Eve and Easter Day* (1850) – one of his least liked, because so meditative, religious poems. But, even there, where he shows his preference for a chapel service over any other, he speaks warmly of God's love, and this corresponds with the overwhelming 'joy' Cleon senses but cannot answer. The main issue at stake, then, is that 'Cleon' seeks to demonstrate that intellectuals who are unable to convert to Christianity may none the less glimpse 'God's divine plan' almost in spite of themselves. Although this may lend poignancy to Cleon's plight, it also serves again to strengthen Browning's position which cannot draw its model of historical development into the kinds of doubt Cleon must suffer. 'Cleon' is wiser than Cleon; and yet 'Cleon' needs Cleon's saddening myopia to make its poetic vision clear.

Repeatedly, Cleon approximates Browning's history of human consciousness. He knows there is a highly developed 'quality' within the human 'soul' (211) that, by virtue of its 'intro-active' (212) nature, enables human beings to become cognisant of the need to know how and why they are alive. This is a 'critical' facility; it enables self-knowledge and growth; and, when used properly, it produces 'joy'. In fact, the word 'joy' hereafter recurs in the poem on numerous occasions taking on increasingly discomfiting tones. Realising that the pursuit of 'joy' is one of the prime motivations of life, Cleon at first tells

Protus that the magnificent tower crowning the islands is but one manifestation of the insatiable human desire to 'struggle . . . enlarge . . . Increase' and 'supply' (245–7) energy in the world around him.

Yet the more he contemplates the expenditure of this desire the more overwhelming it becomes – to the point that it induces near madness. For, as far as Cleon can see, 'life's inadequate to joy' (249). 'Joy' may combine the soul's wisdom with the craving of the flesh, but it redounds to nothing. Sharing Cleon's agony, Protus gives his command: 'Let progress end at once' (222); and argues that 'Most progress is most failure' (272). For the desire to reach towards a level of critical consciousness – how 'Man's spirit might grow conscious of man's life' (220) – undermines the despot's authority; and yet his inquiring mind compels him to search for a solution to his infernal desire. Cleon makes his peroration by stating that humanity has raised itself above 'the brute's head' (230) only to mount a 'tower that crowns a country' (235) and 'perish there' (236). And so Protus' magnificent monument ironically transforms into a symbol of wasted human resources. It represents one despairing phase of human endeavour that should never be returned to. In one of his disputatious 'parleyings', 'With Gerard de Lairesse' (1887), Browning points out why Greek culture had to be superseded. Ancient Greece was the modern world in its infancy:

> Earth's young significance is all to learn:
> The dead Greek lore lies buried in the urn
> Where who seeks fire finds ashes. Ghost, forsooth!
> What was the best Greece babbled of as truth?
>
> (391–4)

Similarly, Cleon ends by imagining himself dead in his urn, with no understanding as to why the insatiable 'joy-hunger' (328) frustrates the intellect. Since Zeus has not revealed his secret to him, Cleon is unable to put Protus' equally agitated mind at rest. The tyrant is so anxious about the meaning of human life that he has sent a messenger to listen to St Paul. Cleon advises Protus not to stoop so low – for a 'barbarian Jew' (343), one who cannot speak Greek, should be despised. This highly accomplished Greek artist, then, may be viewed as a victim of circumstance; his snobbish values have frustrated his understanding of the Christian truth that would calm his soul. Here, perhaps, we see a critique of the perils of Arnoldian Hellenism.

'Cleon', in many ways, echoes the discordant notes struck in Arnold's 'Empedocles on Etna', where the ancient philosopher, disillusioned with the ability of the intellect to answer the aching desires of the soul, climbs the volcano and flings himself into the heart of its hellish fires. The poem, widely regarded as Arnold's greatest, caused him considerable unease, and reveals a telling indecisiveness in the aesthetic choices he was trying to make in the 1850s. First published in 1852, he withdrew it from his *Poems* of the following year. The accompanying 1853 'Preface', a significant document in mid-Victorian poetic theory, outlined his reasons for the exclusion of 'Empedocles'. The poem was, he said, 'painful', not 'tragic'. It came too close to the troubled state of mind that characterised the repugnant present age. Arnold deemed 'Empedocles' faulty because it was too 'morbid' to release the cathartic 'enjoyment' rendered possible even by tragedy. By implication, he was doing a disservice to classical culture. Quoting Schiller, Arnold claims: 'The right art is that alone, which creates the highest enjoyment.'[30] Cleon's obsession with 'joy' would appear to interrogate the form of pleasure that Arnold, and by extension Empedocles, strove for but felt he had not achieved.

Living at a time of cultural crisis, when the sophists (itinerant lecturers) have overrun the schools, Empedocles is faced with a divided world from which he feels irremediably alienated. Few take his wisdom seriously any longer. And those who do, like Pausanias, who accompanies him up the mountainside, are deluded. They turn to Empedocles with their heads full of superstition, wanting to know the secret to the miraculous cures he has administered – one to a woman who had lain in a trance for thirty years. The world, it seems, is populated by a disharmonious band of teachers infamous for their specious argumentation, religious sentimentalists and, finally, hapless myth-makers – like the young harpist, Callicles, whose mellifluous songs aim to soothe Empedocles' conscience, but fail to do so because of their content. Callicles cannot see how badly these stories affect Empedocles' state of mind. Two of Callicles' lyrics unwittingly record acts of brutal violence committed by the gods – Zeus' imprisonment of Typho, whose groans can be heard interminably rumbling beneath Etna; and the torture of Marsyas the faun, flayed alive for challenging Apollo to a musical contest. Each actor in Arnold's dramatic poem has his Victorian double, as Culler points out:

> Just as Callicles recalls the Wordsworthian or Keatsian poet of nature and myth, and just as the sophists who have won the empire in the schools are analogous to the triumphant Utilitarian or positivistic philosophers, so Pausanias is the type of bewildered nineteenth-century clergyman who sees in miracles the focal point in the conflict between science and religion.[31]

Empedocles himself would seem to be Arnold's own disturbing alter ego. The concerns of the 'Preface' parallel those of the philosopher, attempting to recapture the spirit and meaning of 'joy'. Recalling happier times with his teacher, when he could make sense of the world, Empedocles cries out:

> And yet what days were those, Parmenides!
> When we were young, when we could number friends
> In all the Italian cities like ourselves,
> When with elated hearts we joined your train,
> Ye Sun-born Virgins! on the road of truth.

Then we could still enjoy, then neither thought
Nor outward things were closed and dead to us;
But we received the shock of mighty thoughts
On simple minds with a pure natural joy;
And if the sacred load oppressed our brain,
We had the power to feel the pressure eased,
The brow unbound, the thoughts flow free again,
In the delightful commerce of the world.
We had not lost our balance then, nor grown
Thought's slaves, and dead to every natural joy.

(II. 235–49)

Since lines such as these suggest strong intertextual connections with 'Cleon', it is worth asking exactly what kind of
response Browning's poem is making to both 'Empedocles on
Etna' and the 'Preface' which dispensed with it in the 1853
volume.

Arnold's 'Preface', like Empedocles, looks longingly at better
days gone by for a sense of completeness, permanence and
greatness: 'Achilles, Prometheus, Clytemnestra, Dido – what
modern poem presents personages as interesting, even to us
moderns, as these personages of an "exhausted past"?'[32]
Although Arnold asserts the 'modernness or antiquity of an
action . . . has nothing to do with its fitness for poetical
representation', he expresses a strong preference for classical
poetry, since it exhibits those actions which express 'elemen-
tary feelings which subsist permanently in the race'. These
'permanent passions' are altogether greater than the contingent
preoccupations of modern poetry which, in the words of one
Victorian reviewer cited by Arnold, focuses on 'the state of
one's own mind in a representative history'. The reviewer in
question, David Masson, was praising, not blaming, modern
poets for their researches into the mind. Quoting Masson in
this way, Arnold was making a slighting remark against the
fashionable 'Spasmodic' school of poets – Sydney Dobell,

Philip James Bailey and Alexander Smith, to name the main trio – whose highly discursive psychological poems caught the public's attention in the 1850s, and whose stylistic idiosyncracies were famously satirised by a number of commentators. He saw 'Spasmodic' poems, in their wildly exclamatory mode, manifesting the 'confusion of the present times', and he derives their sensationalism from faults characterising Shakespeare's writing, and which turn up, in more recent form, in Keats's 'Isabella, or the Pot of Basil' (1820).

To Arnold, English poetry seemed generally in disarray, and Browning may well have been thought partly responsible for this. Bailey modelled his most popular work, *Festus* (1839), on Browning's *Paracelsus*, and Dobell emulated aspects of Browning's style. These 'spasms' affected others as well. Tennyson appropriated 'Spasmodic' infelicities in his maniacal monodrama, *Maud*. For Arnold, modern English poetry was placing too much emphasis on qualities that could only impair art: vicissitudes of mind; formal incoherence; and superficial picturesque details. Worst of all, such poems attended to history, not action; they probed individual foibles, not universal conditions. Bewildered, like Empedocles, Arnold ultimately claims that the 'only sure guidance, the only solid footing' lies among 'the ancients'. In these lights, Cleon may begin to sound rather like Arnold himself, with the ghost of Empedocles not far behind. Where Arnold, Empedocles and Cleon turn their gaze to the earliest and purest forms of classical culture, Browning's 'Cleon' looks obliquely at the religion that shall supersede it – for Christianity holds the key to forms of historical understanding that would not celebrate the ancients as unsurpassable in achievement, but rather located their labours as one phase in an on-going process. The debate here, therefore, is between Browning's historicism and Arnold's classicism.

'Empedocles' filled Browning with admiration, and he urged Arnold to reprint it in the 1867 edition of *Poems* (which Arnold duly did). Why? It formed part of a friendly argument with

Arnold's classicism that lasted well into the 1870s – in both Browning's preface to his translation of the *Agamemnon of Aeschylus* (1873) and his long disquisition on the merits of forms of classical comedy and tragedy, *Aristophanes' Apology* (1875).[33] This colloquy may have initially been prompted by Arnold's covert attack in 'Empedocles' on Browning's 'Saul' – first published, in incomplete form, in 1845. Culler sees this as 'barely possible', but notes that the poem of Browning's 'which most closely resembles "Empedocles of Etna" is "Saul", where a youthful harp-player very much like Callicles tries to relieve the gloom of an aged king very much like Empedocles . . . By the Christian argument Saul is restored, whereas Empedocles dies in his volcano.'[34]

This tangential link with 'Saul', which Browning expanded, and drew to its visionary conclusion in 1855, points to the role of miracles in Christianity, which the Higher Critics, in much the same way as Empedocles, disputed, seeking rational explanations for them. In the Old Testament, Saul's harp song performs a typological function – that is, it anticipates crucial events in Christ's life. Relations between Old Testament types and their New Testament counterparts, anti-types, are central to the interpretative activity of Browning's biblical poems. They accentuate those structures of future expectation that shape Browning's aesthetic, and further explain his differences from Arnold.

'Saul', in both the 1845 and 1855 versions, is saturated with typological symbolism, and the title of the series of eight pamphlets in which it first appeared was, so to speak, true to type. The naming of *Bells and Pomegranates* was not entirely clear to Elizabeth Barrett, and it may have been for this reason that he appended the following note to the final number:

> I only meant by that title to indicate an endeavour towards something like an alternation, or mixture, of music with discoursing, sound with sense, poetry with thought; which looks too

ambitious, thus expressed, so the symbol was preferred. It is little to the purpose, that such is actually one of the most familiar of the many Rabbinical (and Patristic) acceptations of the phrase.

Barrett knew that these items were embroidered alternately on the hem of high priest's robe (Exodus 28: 33–4) but she could not grasp Browning's use of them. Browning wrongly assumed that his educated audience would have instantly recognised the prefigurative purpose of this religious garment. The high priest was a type of Christ. And so, by inference, Browning's title indicates the prophetic role of poetry. The bells and pomegranates serve, as he says, an additional function – to point to the mixture of styles present here. As Linda H. Peterson observes: 'The plays and the new dramatic monologues' comprising this innovative series of pamphlets 'are not direct utterances, but "sweet sounds" which remind the reader of some truth already known and thus carry with them the promise of fruit.'[35] Having heard the ironic resonances of the speaker's words, the audience is put in a position to reap the hidden truths that the poet–prophet has implanted there. It may appear that reading a dramatic monologue is analogous to typological exegesis: first, images are found, then transformed into types, and lastly shaped into a forward looking history. This, at least, would seem to be the hermeneutic process implied by the title.

But Browning's use of types was not so programmatic and neither was the exegetical tradition on which he drew, as Adrienne Munich states: 'The concept of types – as in emblems and as in biblical typology – is a confused and confusing tradition. Since it came down to Browning through his own reading, through his listening to sermons, and by following a characteristic mode of thought of his times it cannot be ordered into an internally coherent system.'[36] 'Saul' is so richly patterned with typological meanings that Browning goes so far as to invent types of his own. For example, the incident to

which the opening lines are not recorded in 1 Samuel 16:
14–23, which chronicles the story of the two great Israelite
kings, David and Saul. In the 1855 version, Saul's brother,
Abner, is reported as having said the following:

> 'Since the King, O my friend, for thy countenance sent,
> Neither drunken nor eaten have we; nor until from his tent
> Thou return with the joyful assurance the King liveth yet,
> Shall our lip with the honey be bright, with the water be
> wet.
> For out of the black mid-tent's silence, a space of three
> days,
> Not a sound hath escaped to thy servants, of prayer nor of
> praise,
> To betoken that Saul and the Spirit have ended their
> strife.'
>
> (3–9)

No such event exists in the first book of Samuel. Yet Browning
has devised it to anticipate the three days Christ spent in the
tomb before the Resurrection. There is a clear correspondence
between the two events.

Less immediate is the link between Saul's battle with the evil
spirit and Christ's agony in the garden. And, indeed, much of
Browning's poem picks up on biblical motifs that suggest more
than confirm typological symbols. Ward Hellstrom has enu-
merated many of these types.[37] David typifies Christ's anoint-
ment since he is graced with 'dew' (11) on his 'gold hair' (12).
Later, David takes up the role of the shepherd, playing 'the
tune all our sheep know' (36) – an image that not only Christ
will fulfil but that is also prefigured in the non-canonical Jewish
apocalypses. The key point here is that Saul, the first King of
Israel, embodies or iconises, Christ's salvation of humanity in
the crucifixion. As David looks up at his elder, he sees Saul
'erect as that tent-prop, both arms stretched out wide/On the

121

great cross support in the centre, that goes to each side' (28–9). And this image prompts David's revelatory vision: 'See the Christ stand!' (312). David can disclose God's typological designs on earth by inferring the forms of evolutionary progress around him. Addressing Saul, he says:

> 'In our flesh grows the branch of this life, in our soul
>> it bears fruit.
> Thou hast marked the slow rise of the tree, – how its stem
>> trembled first
> Till is passed the kid's lip, the stag's antler; then
>> safely outburst
> The fan-branches all round; and thou mindest when these
>> too, in turn
> Broke a-bloom and the palm-tree seemed perfect'
>> (150–5)

Once again, Browning's historical outlook is accentuated by a Lamarckian interest in the desirous 'branching' of life from lower to higher forms. Yet there is also another model of understanding in play here, and this is the analogical reasoning performed by 'natural theology' – laid out extensively by William Paley in *Natural Theology* (1802) and by Bishop Butler in *Analogy of Religion* (1730). Both took this method for understanding natural phenomena as God's work on earth from Newton's *Principia* (1687). Butler's teaching was highly influential in the universities, and it seems to filter into Browning's work wherever he is looking for principles of congruity between seemingly disparate elements – such as a tree and a deer. This form of analysis is explicitly referred to in the subtitle to 'Caliban upon Setebos' (1864), Browning's reimagining of the colonialist fantasy in Shakespeare's *The Tempest*. Caliban, too, comes close to making sense of God's plan – but, as the kind of 'native' subjected to increasingly close scrutiny by Victorian anthropologists, Caliban creates a violent religion for himself. He builds a destructive god, Setebos, out of his own brutal impulses. In his own savage myth making Caliban asserts that Setebos tricks and punishes nature just as cruelly as he does; here he is discussing how he has trapped a bird:

'I catch the birds, I am the crafty thing,
I make the cry my maker cannot make
With his great round mouth; he must blow through mine!'
Would I not smash it with my foot? So He.

(123–6)

It is possible to argue that 'Caliban upon Setebos' satirises natural theology as a misguided form of reasoning, leading to a view of God as one who arbitrarily punishes his victims. But Caliban's errors are more the obverse of those of his civilised counterparts, such as Cleon and David. Michael Timko observes that, in Caliban, Browning 'is indicating how lack of faith in man's intuitive recognition of God and his ignoring the doctrine of revelation, through which means God revealed Himself to man, are the real enemies to true faith'.[38] Caliban, imaging Setebos with his 'great round mouth' (note the racist connotations), is yet another figure on the ascending ladder of knowledge. He, like Cleon, can glimpse a realm of calm which he calls the 'Quiet', and this is a distant vision of the Christian God – one who reigns over, and who will finally conquer, the relentless damage inflicted on the world by Setebos. Gillian Beer writes: 'The shifty, revelatory quality of analogy aligns it to magic',[39] and this would seem to be in keeping with the joint movement of typology and historicism in these poems – whereby each image can be placed within a fictive design that may approximate God's overarching plan of human progress. All this goes to show that where natural and religious histories are concerned, Browning's work is compounded of many elements. But each tradition he draws on has at its centre a belief in transformation. Witnessing the raising of Lazarus, Karshish (another imaginary figure) nearly converts to Christianity. In his 'Epistle' (1855), this Arab physician comes to understand how this miraculous event, which he at first explains to himself as a form of 'epilepsy' (80), opened heaven 'on a soul while yet on earth' while 'Earth forced on a soul's use while seeing heaven' (141–2).

Miracles, like history, did not require scientific evidence for Browning. Revelation did not depend on fact but imagination, and this point emerges in the most complex, if doggedly doctrinal, of Browning's biblical poems, 'A Death in the Desert' (1864). For here Christianity is taken to mythological extremes, not as a test of faith, but as a challenge to Renan, and his demeaning attitude towards John's Gospel. Both Strauss, in *The Life of Jesus* (widely available in George Eliot's translation of 1845), and Renan in his *Life of Jesus* (1863) agreed that John's record of Christ's life deviated from the narrative re-counted by Matthew, Mark, and Luke. But where Strauss was willing to confirm his own faith on the basis of Christianity as myth, Renan dismissed Christ's works as fraudulent, and mocked John's idealisation of himself as the most favoured apostle. Renan sees John as a spurious chronicler, one who gives himself undue pride of place among the Lord's closest followers:

> John, after the death of Jesus, appears in fact to have received the mother of his master into his house, and to have adopted her (John 19: 27). The great consideration which Mary enjoyed in the early church, doubtless led John to pretend that Jesus, whose favourite disciple he wished to be regarded, had, when dying, recommended to his care all that was dearest to him. The presence of this precious trust near John, insured him a kind of precedence over the other apostles, and gave his doctrine high authority.[40]

Browning contests such aspersions against John's integrity by devising a scene where John himself expresses anxiety about the authority of the divine logos, and how this may vanish with him. E. S. Shaffer states that Browning takes up Renan's challenge on the critic's own psychological ground.[41] He is the last of the apostles and so, it would seem, the final curator of God's word: '"Since James and Peter had release by death/ . . . I am only he, your brother John, / Who saw and heard, and could remember all"' (115–17). Throughout, he is concerned that his book '"cannot pass"' (368); that is, he is worried that his words will be mistrusted without him. Alive, he is able to declare '"I saw"' (133). Dead, his book '"speaks on"' (368), but at the hands of potential doubters. His worry is with authenticity and immediacy. Yet, as these two sets of quotation marks show, John's voice is surrounded by a frame. Browning has carefully set up his poem to disclose that John's words have been transcribed and retranscribed so many times that it proves difficult to accord much authority to them. The poem is prefaced with remarks about the origination of the text. One who cryptically signs himself with '*Epsilon*' and '*Mu*' (9), reports that John's speech was 'Supposed of Pamphylax the Antiochene' (1) who may have inherited it from Xanthus – and Xanthus, it later appears, 'could not write the chronicle' (56). Such subversive documents, in any case, had to be kept hidden from the Romans.

Against Renan, Browning uses his imaginary John to observe that Christ's miracles were instrumental in bringing men and women within sight of '"God the Truth"' (431), and having borne the necessary '"fruit"' (443), they were promptly dispensed with. There was no need for further proof: '"that miracle was duly wright/When, save for it, no faith was possible"' (464–6). Indeed, Browning makes John responsible for those actions that Renan identified to reveal the apostle's deceitfulness. Renan claimed that John makes his presence at the Crucifixion far too prominent; Browning's John admits that when he saw the '"sudden Roman faces"' (308) he fled the scene. Browning's strategy is to make every weakness Renan imputes to John into one of the saint's main strengths. He goes so far as to let John claim that he, a mere apostle, performed a miracle, restoring sight to a blind man (459–60). Such a claim ostensibly draws the truth of John's Gospel into question in a more far reaching manner than Renan's criticism.

But in this satirical attack on Renan, John gives voice to a view of history that extends greatly beyond matters of textual detail. John states more clearly, and dogmatically, than any of Browning's personae that the revelation of divine truth was performed in stages, and each phase of human history inched towards the God who had set it in motion. Moses, for example, passed on God's commandments on the tablets of stone received on Mount Horeb, anticipating Christ's teaching. These stones were '"replaced as time requires"' (628), for each epoch struggles to '"reach the type!"' (629). This is a history structured upon a progressive principle of trial and error:

> 'God's gift was that man should conceive of truth
> And yearn to gain it, catching at mistake,
> As midway help till he reach fact indeed.'
>
> (605–7)

This philosophy is not bound to textual evidence. The 'fact' of it transcends the inevitably erroneous material word. For it is the myth of Christ and his apostles that communicates the spirit of God's love, touches the soul, and thereby brings men and women closer to divinity. Such views were gaining a wider purchase in the 1840s. As Elizabeth Barrett observed, 'Christianity is a worthy *myth*, and poetically acceptable.'[42] It had to be respected as a fiction. And, in that, 'A Death in the Desert' is a piece of Victorian myth making, practising exactly what it preaches. Browning's form, then, is John's theme.

In his final volume, *Asolando* (1889), Browning made one of his clearest statements about the imaginative element involved in all forms of historical understanding. 'Development' records his growing historical consciousness, from his childhood, when his father arranged his toys to explain the siege of Troy, to his later engagement with Friedrich August Wolf's *Prolegomena in Homerum* (1795), which made the powerful argument that Homer's writings were probably by diverse hands, having been handed down through an oral tradition. At first, he was unsettled by the idea of there being 'No actual Homer, no authentic text' (70). But, on reflection, he learnt that the 'dream' (84) he had come to love, in all its heroic endeavour, was valuable precisely because of its fictive quality. It was this that reanimated 'Helen, Ulysses, Hector and his Spouse, / Achilles and his friend' (81–2). Had his father denied him this 'mythology' (95), and given him Aristotle's Ethics instead (which seems dry by comparison), he would have not been able to have written his poem – and, by implication, all his poetry. For the purpose of myth lies in its power to dramatise events that may have no historical basis in fact. Instead, they are made to happen through the activity of poetry. In this, Browning's characters from the Italian Renaissance and the earliest years of Christianity are just as real as those found in other records. History is ultimately a story. But it was not one to be told in an arbitrary manner. That history was, indeed, a story – shaped and enabled by God – remained the all-encompassing narrative which Browning, in his own fictions, had to tell.

4

Lovers

Browning produced some of the most searching love poems of
the nineteenth century, and questions of gender and sexuality
are very much to the fore of his writing. His continuing preoccupation with erotic themes, both male and female sexual
desire, forms part of a general trend within bourgeois Victorian
poetry. All the major poets turned their attentions to issues of
sexual attraction and repulsion, if not violence. More forcefully
than any other discourse of the time, poetry opened up a space
where the awkward tensions between sexual longing and being
could be closely investigated. Where sexuality is concerned,
Victorian poets take risks, and Browning is one of the most
adventurous. On the face of it his views on relations between
the sexes are liberal-minded and egalitarian. For him sexual
acts bear no shame. They are a source of celebration for he
views heterosexual love as one of God's greatest gifts to men
and women. So he urges its revelation, not concealment.
Everyone should be able to recognise the attraction between
men and women, he argues. But, as this chapter shows, in
championing the spirit of individualism and equal partnership

in love, Browning has his masculine biases. Masculinity and femininity – which he recognised as determined opposites – are continuously in conflict with his firm commitment to the liberal subject: a free, independent and ostensibly ungendered being.

Gender and individualism were often at odds, in both his life and writing. It may be surprising to learn that in 1885 he was considering writing a five-act play against women's suffrage. He was, after all, married for sixteen years to one of the most outspoken women poets of the age. As one modern feminist critic of Barrett Browning's writing has pointed out, marriage actually made her work more confident in exploring ideals of independent womanhood and supportive sisterhood,[1] and her rejoicing in female empowerment echoes in several poems in *Men and Women*. Her greatest work, *Aurora Leigh* (1856), draws on the resources of an earlier generation of women poets, notably Felicia Hemans, Caroline Norton and Letitia E. Landon, to show the victory of the female will in a sexually hypocritical and inescapably patriarchal society. Browning's own work often sympathises with the needs of independent women, as analyses of several of his poems of 1855 and 1864 in this chapter seek to demonstrate. Nina Auerbach, by contrast, has argued that much of Browning's canon is given over to laying his wife's ghost to rest, often in oblique and disturbing forms.[2] But the passage from their intertwined biographies to their poetic intertextuality may lead to some confusion. Images of the Brownings in print and in person often vary enormously.

There were certainly disagreements between this generally happily married couple, and 'Mr Sludge the Medium' (1864) and *Prince Hohenstiel-Schwangau* (1871), both published after her death, mock two of Barrett Browning's enthusiasms. 'Mr Sludge' mercilessly sends up the charlatan spiritualist who plays tricks on vulnerable minds; Sludge is the barely disguised alias of the American Daniel Home whose seance the Brownings had attended in 1855, and which thoroughly outraged Browning. Spirit rapping created a minor breach between them and made Barrett Browning discourage her correspondents from mentioning the topic. Browning's prince is similarly distasteful. A demagogue who uses his rhetorical charm in an attempt to seduce his young lady auditor, he immediately invites comparisons with Barrett Browning's beloved Napoleon III, whose troops invaded Italy in 1859. Her penultimate volume, *Poems before Congress* (1860), uninhibitedly sings his praises. It aroused considerable hostility from several periodical reviewers, who were unable to see how and why she could lend such support to the emperor in the cause of unifying Italy.

These poems remained sources of anger and embarrassment to Browning, although his own feelings about the emperor varied throughout the 1860s.[3] In the 1850s, however, he showed little trust in Napoleon III's opportunistic policies. From the time of the pan-European revolutions of 1848, which Browning witnessed from very close quarters, he had differed sharply from Barrett Browning's admiration for Napoleon III. In a letter to a friend, she wrote: 'Robert and I have had some domestic *émeutes*, because he hates some imperial names.'[4] And yet, set against this, there is all the passion and large-heartedness of the courtship correspondence, and the loving tribute he makes in 'One Word More' (1855) to the considerable debt he owes Barrett Browning. The intricate conversation – the echoes, transcriptions, silencings – between the Brownings' poems is still not altogether clear.[5] Perhaps, in 1885 – when Browning was in his seventies, and certainly not in his dotage – late Victorian feminist agitation for the vote proved the ultimate test of his long-held and fond attachment to the image of the noble male rescuer: a chivalrous Perseus to an enchained Andromeda. This motif is scattered in many places in his writing, all the way from *Pauline* to *Parleyings with Certain People of Importance in Their Day*, and his marriage may appear to be shaped by this legend – except when we begin to understand how Barrett Browning, and not Browning himself, had to take charge of her escape from Wimpole Street, and sort out the times of ferries to France.

His sexual attitudes, if progressive, were riven with contradictions, the most amusing of which concern Browning's impassioned defences of the female nude in painting and sculpture. To represent a woman's body in this way, was as he saw it, the divine prerogative of male artists. Here, in 'With Francis Furini', he imagines the painter with whom he is 'parleying' expressing an assured sense of satisfaction at having done God's work in depicting the female body, and this prompts Browning to recall his cherished classical myth:

> I trust
> . . . Furini, dying breath had vent
> In some fine fervour of thanksgiving just
> For this – that soul and body's power you spent –
> Agonized to adumbrate, trace in dust
> That marvel which we dream the firmament
> Copies in star-device when fancies stray
> Outlining, orb by orb, Andromeda –
> God's best of beauteous and magnificent
> Revealed to earth – the naked female form.
>   (134–43)

A group of poems, including ones from *Pacchiarotto and How He Worked in Distemper* (1876) and *Asolando* (1889), rail against the narrow-minded opinions of minor eighteenth-century art critic and painter, Filippo Baldinucci, especially the opprobrium Baldinucci cast on supposedly immoral representations of the nude. In this passage, Browning's impatience with Baldinucci compounds his irritation with John Callcot Horsley, treasurer of the Royal Academy, who expressed his distaste for the huge nude sculptures produced by Pen Browning (by then in his late thirties). But, as Ann P. Brady points out: 'The vehemence of Browning's defence and his attribution of evil-in-the-eye-of-the beholder to Furini's or Pen's critics is amazing

131

in one who, from childhood through manhood, considered it
the worst possible calamity to be seen in a state of undress.'[6]

Browning's view of the female nude and female sexuality was
never explicitly salacious. But he drew freely on images of
orgasm and penetration that have a pornographic element.
The woman's body may be a site of purity in its nakedness. Yet
it is also a place where the male eye may focus on sources of
sexual excitement. Indeed, the male gaze, sensing a somewhat
hydraulic force of eroticism, often finds itself in conflict with
the liberal ethic of individual freedom to which so many of his
best known poems are espoused. Take, for example, these lines
from the dizzyingly lyrical 'Women and Roses' (1855):

I

I dream of a red rose-tree.
And which of its roses three
Is the dearest rose to me?

II

Round and round, like a dance of snow
In a dazzling drift, as its guardians, go
Floating the women faded for ages,
Sculptured in stone, on the poet's pages.
Then follow women fresh and gay,
Living and loving and loved to-day.
Last, in the rear, flee the multitude of maidens,
Beauties yet unborn. And all, to one cadence,
They circle their rose on my tree.

. . . .

IV

Stay then, stoop, since I cannot climb,
You, great shapes of the antique time!
How shall I fix you, fire you, freeze you,

Break my heart at your feet to please you?
Oh, to possess and be possessed!
Hearts that beat 'neath each pallid breast!
Once but of love, the poesy, the passion,
Drink but once and die! – In vain, the same fashion,
They circle their rose on my rose tree.
                                    (1–12, 16–24)

This poem, as its title clearly indicates, is making some fairly commonplace connections between flowers and femininity. Women, like roses, are prized for their beauty. First, they are buds, then they flourish, and finally, once their 'term is reached' (13), they wither. The rose, therefore, provides an image of potential defloration, and, more specifically still, it is a metaphor for the vagina. For in the rose's 'ruby-rimmed . . . nectar-brimmed' (26–7) petals lies its male partner, the bee. But the bee cannot languish in this female organ. If this is a place of male sexual 'yearning' (31), and intercourse leading to conception ('Thy bud's the babe unborn' (38)), it is also, confoundingly, a zone of death. Students of the English Renaissance know only too well that to 'die' in John Donne's poetry (which Browning also knew well) means to ejaculate. Coition mortifies desires that forever seek, as desires do, to be fulfilled.

Throughout 'Women and Roses', the male imagination is littered with an unstoppable 'dazzling drift' of female forms, from ones 'Sculptured in stone' to others depicted 'on the poet's pages'. Even when, breathtakingly, the woman's 'cincture slips' (33) beneath her waist, promising the man 'eternities of pleasure' (34), he remains ultimately unsatisfied. A pageant of female forms continues to 'circle' in his mind. Much as he would like to 'fix', 'fire', and 'freeze' the woman of his dreams, he recognises what it means to 'Drink but once and die'. The will 'to possess and be possessed', a fantasy of mutual union, is continually thwarted by its own compulsive energies. Since the conjunction of 'women and roses' is so overproductive of meaning, it is not surprising that he prays for 'Wings' (40) to lift him out of his misery. His final plea is loaded with castration anxiety: 'I will make an Eve, be the artist that began her,/ Shaped her to his mind! – Alas! in like manner/They circle their rose on my rose tree' (46–8). It is not only that women cannot be overmastered – as if this were simply an inevitable psychic structure. The point of the poem would seem to be an ethical one too: that women should not be entrapped by a man's all consuming desire. Women have the right to resist a male impulse that seeks to 'fix' its object. Although the Penguin editors quietly suggest that 'Women and Roses' is 'most uncharacteristic of its author'[7] (they sound rather shocked by it), it does in fact point to a number of difficulties that repeatedly confront the male lover in Browning's poetry. Examined carefully, the poem reveals how the male imagination is trying to cope with a concept of femininity that is at once, and contradictorily, magnetic, superabundant and, moreover, autonomous. His projection of woman, somehow, outstrips his capacity to reconcile himself to her. Perhaps we should assume that only God, and not mortal men, has the prerogative to make woman in His image?

If in 'Women and Roses' the man declares he is unable to 'climb' to the heights on which his image of woman stands (for he believes he is her inferior), and which obliges him to ask her to 'stoop' down to him (for his heart is breaking), 'Two in the Campagna', also from Men and Women, examines with similar intensity the problem of making love on equal terms. It is in this poem that Browning concentrates on his doctrine of the elusive 'infinite moment', here figured as the 'good minute' (50), in which true love can only momentarily thrive. The ejaculatory 'good minute' is not easily sustained, and it represents an attenuated and distinctly Victorian form of the sublime. From the outset, the male speaker (and I am assuming it is a man who is trying to 'pluck the rose' (48))[8] opens with a gentle enquiry to find out whether his erotic feelings are shared

by his female partner. His tone is open, questioning, explora-
tory: 'I wonder do you feel to-day/ As I have felt since, hand in
hand,/We sat down on the grass . . .' (1–3). Expressing such
emotions, in the hope they will be requited, involves complex
processes of ideation. To make his case, he traces the shape of
his hesitant thoughts across the contours of the Roman landscape where he first enjoyed the woman's company. One thing
is very clear in his figurative use of the campagna. He is keen
not to idealise love. For that would betray its immediate
physical reality. In this poem, Browning interrogates the
premises upon which traditional landscape poetry is based. In
'Two in the Campagna', he is drawing upon, and radically
modifying, the loco-descriptive styles of eighteenth-century
pastoral. In his hands, a once green, fecund and passively
consoling nature transforms into a strikingly colourful prospect
where the forces of life and death are busily disturbing one
another: the campagna is both gaudy and gothic. And the
sensory qualities of the poem are arresting, because they
combine in unexpected ways. Having tried, and failed, to catch
a spider's web, he watches it drift on the breeze before him. The
web iconises the sexual feelings he is trying to express, and
which, like gossamer, seem ungraspable:

> First it left
> The yellowing fennel, run to seed
> There, branching from the brickwork's cleft,
> Some old tomb's ruin: yonder weed
> Took up the floating weft,
>
> Where one small orange cup massed
> Five beetles, – blind and green they grope
> Among the honey-meal: and last,
> Everywhere on the grassy slope
> I traced it. Hold it fast!
>
> (11–20)

Even if the spider's web is tantalisingly beyond his reach, he enjoys witnessing its gradual progress across this scene. (In other words, he knows that there are things passing before his gaze which he can never fully comprehend – the structure of negativity again.) Features of landscape are provocatively incongruous. For here a ruin is a seeding ground. Likewise, a cup of decaying honey-meal provides a feast for ravenous insects. By intermixing fertility and decay, and thus going against tradition, this description is an attempt at realism. Here, nature is at its most elemental – with weeds and beetles, not meadows and sheep. And, as the next two stanzas show, the 'champaign with its endless fleece' (21) is where sexual, rather than romantic, love may be imagined:

> Such life here, through such lengths of hours,
>   Such miracles performed in play,
> Such primal naked forms of flowers,
>   Such letting nature have her way
> While heaven looks from its towers!
>
> How say you? Let us, O my dove,
>   Let us be unashamed of soul,
> As earth lies bare to heaven above!
>   How is it under our control
> To love or not to love?
>
> (26–35)

The campagna is a kind of Eden where 'primal naked forms', not just flowers, but also Adam and Eve, once existed in harmony with everything around them. Forever true to God's wishes, sexual desire has never been corrupted by the Fall. Eroticism is viewed as a divinely ordained response, a miraculous reenactment and expression of His love, and so men and women must be 'unashamed' in their passion. Yet, in saying this, the male speaker has to negotiate the erotic very carefully. Victorian propriety remains, as does a slight sentimentalism

('O my dove'). Flowers and the earth can only be thought of as 'naked' and 'bare' instead of human flesh. But, for all these tactful obliquities, 'Two in the Campagna' is still, for its time, a courageous poem in revising – as much as it is able – conventional representations of sexual love.

Before he may 'pluck the rose', which is in both formal and sexual terms the climax of the poem, he grows worryingly conscious of a confounding 'fault' (39) between them. Even if God encourages the lovers to be 'unashamed' (it is His will, not theirs), the speaker is troubled by the potential inequalities of love. Guided towards this divine act of sexual union, he none the less fears violating the woman's individuality. Each clause amplifies this tension: 'I would that you were all to me, / You that are just so much, no more. / Nor yours nor mine, nor slave nor free' (36–8). Asserting the conventional demand that she should surrender her will to him, he instantly negates that claim. He would like 'all' of her but not if that means her subjection. To counter the implications of this sentiment, he then decides that since she can never be 'all' to him, she is inevitably 'just so much'. But this may sound rather insensitive, as if he is belittling her. So the next line offers some kind of resolution through a run of negatives to obliterate all notions of possession whatsoever.

It is hardly insignificant that he briefly alludes to slavery. Both Brownings came from families who had turned their backs on slave owning holdings in the West Indies, and slavery receives polemical treatment in Barrett Browning's work: her best known poem on this topic, 'The Runaway Slave at Pilgrim's Point' (1847), was commissioned by the Anti-Slavery Bazaar in Boston. Browning would have been aware how closely Barrett Browning connected women's lives to the plight of American slaves, still not emancipated until the time of the Civil War, shortly after her death. The metaphor of slavery was widely used by women writers (it recurs throughout Charlotte Brontë's *Jane Eyre* (1847)), and by political radicals. It had been applied to the subjection of the British working classes from the early 1830s; Richard Oastler's letters of protest to the *Leeds Mercury* are the most famous examples.[9] Browning's liberalism is certainly in a quandary here, since his speaker would seem to want to do away with both slavery *and* freedom. For to be free would mean independence to the degree of not being able to 'possess or be possessed' by another. This is the dilemma of the liberal individual in love. So he wants to know 'What the core/O' the wound, since wound must be?' (39–40). This centre of pain is also the seat of passion ('core' as the French '*coeur*' or Italian '*cora*'). There is no undoing this paradox – it persists right to the end of the poem.

Even when he imagines the moment of consummation, he places it in a hypothetical context: the conditional tense governs his conflicting impulses to be at one with, and yet autonomous from, his lover: 'I would I could adopt your will' (41). The most he can manage is to 'touch' her 'close' (46), and then 'stand away' (47). Such hesitant feelings suggest, at once, a fussily chivalrous sensibility and a tetchily masculine defensiveness. This doubling of tone is important. Once out of the 'good minute', he compares himself to a barbed yet free and easy 'thistle-ball' (53), at the mercy of 'light winds' (54). His seed is 'Fixed by no friendly star' (55). Post-coital triste leaves him abandoned, suggesting, perhaps, that he feels betrayed. Such despondency is, once more, the 'old trick' (58). Thus he ends as he began, trying to find a 'thread' (57) through the webbed intricacies of his emotions. Yet for all his fears for her right to freedom and the risk of her subjection, the woman remains barely visible. 'Two in the Campagna' is weighted towards the one who speaks it. His plight supersedes hers. Although he makes an opening gesture to find out how she may 'feel to-day', it is how he has 'felt since' that preoccupies him.

'Love among the Ruins', which originally opened the first edition of *Men and Women*, follows a similar structure, and has the same biases, although it makes rather different points about sexual desire in a world of inequalities. Here, love is said to transcend 'whole centuries of folly, noise, and sin' (81), particularly the repeated 'glory' and 'shame' (33, 35) of former generations. Browning is thinking of classical Rome when 'chariots . . . raced, / And the monarch and his minions and his dames / Viewed the games' (46–7). Rome was built on such displays of power, ones hardly to Browning's highly principled democratic tastes. The poem witnesses the decline of the Roman empire, where now a 'single little turret' (37) is all that is left of 'a tower' which 'in ancient time / Sprang sublime' (43–4). Yet it is not only Rome that has diminished in grandeur. The Romantic sublime, once more, has been cut down to size. And pastoral, too, has transmogrified into a scene where 'the country does not even boast a tree' (12). Razed, flattened, matted, these bare Roman hillsides compare, in some ways, with the landscape that reveals Browning's most violent reaction against the Romantics' legacy – the eerie interior of 'Childe Roland to the Dark Tower Came' (1855). Although there is some sparse 'verdure' (15) in this scene, the 'caper' is conspicuously 'overrooted' (39), and the only flower to flourish is an ugly 'patching houseleek's head of blossom' (41). And yet, in compensation, the 'quiet-coloured eve / Smiles' (49–50), and the 'many-tinkling fleece' (51) make their way home 'In such peace' (52). Amid this untamed and uncultivated nature, there are a number of scattered things that can be treasured, and the most significant of them is sexual love.

Love, then, is to be dissociated from the domineering 'Lust' (33) of imperialism, and orthodox poetic idealisation. It redeems humanity. Triumphing over the empires of days gone by, love dispenses with easy lyricism. Metrically, the poem is broken up by strongly marked pauses at the beginning of every five-beat line. Each of these is cut across by a short doubly stressed one. It makes for highly unusual – because so obviously interrupted – rhythms. Both content and form, therefore, affront tradition. So it follows that the woman he pursues waits for him in 'the turret whence the charioteers caught soul/For the goal' (57–8); she presides where the 'monarch and his minions' once thrived. Their rendezvous there provides a complete contrast with the races between sportsmen in the Roman amphitheatres, and the warring armies who sought possession of the land:

> When I do come, she will speak out, she will stand,
>   Either hand
> On my shoulder, give her eyes the first embrace
>   Of my face,
> Ere we rush, ere we extinguish sight and speech
>   Each on each.
>
>   (67–72)

Equable, peaceable, and at one, these lovers repair the wrongs of history. But the poem does not end there. Before he concludes triumphantly that 'Love is best!' (84), he recalls, once more, the violence of war: 'In one year they sent a million fighters forth,/South and North' (73–4). The spectre of battle will not disappear. At the time of composition, one can see why. Lucas suggests that the 'million fighters' refers tangentially to the Crimean War that began in 1854, and witnessed the loss of thousands of British lives.[10] Browning was certainly incensed, as were many Britons, at Prime Minister Aberdeen's military mismanagement, and the all too evident incompetence of the commanding officers.[11] The army was a bastion of aristocratic privilege. But, even if the 'million fighters' covertly allude to British troops perilously rushing to the defence of Turkey, the poem lays its main emphasis on making, as well as resisting, connections between the sexual energies that build empires and those of heterosexuality. The Romans, after all, manifested 'Lust'; their chariots raced around 'a burning ring' (45). Flames of passion similarly fire the lovers' hearts, since they seek – in a livid verb – to 'extinguish' one another. No wonder he reflects on the contradictory aspect of love – 'Oh heart! oh blood that freezes, blood that burns!' (79). In the process of estranging eroticism from imperialism, perhaps Browning is recognising their mutual implication? What act of war might the male speaker be committing on the woman who awaits him?

For love is precarious. The passions that overpower it can be dangerous, as 'A Lovers' Quarrel' (1855) shows. This poem is distinctive because it makes the element of sexual fantasy more prominent than elsewhere in Browning's canon. The male speaker fondly recalls the time he spent with his lover in their snow-bound home. They played games to make light of the bad weather:

> We would try and trace
> One another's face
> In the ash, as an artist draws;
> Free on each other's flaws,
> How we chattered like two church daws!
> (24–8)

Imprisoned in this way, they had an unusual opportunity to explore their freedom together – enough to caricature one another. As Armstrong says: 'The point about these games is not that they were silly, creating factitious thrills, but that every one of them is the model of the continual, free, un-abashed creating of one another that goes on between two people.'[12] Trying to imagine what it might be like to be the other, they were sufficiently uninhibited to cross-dress:

> Teach me to flirt a fan
> As the Spanish ladies can,
> Or I tint your lip
> With a burnt stick's tip
> And you turn into such a man!

> Just the two spots that span
> Half the bill of the young male swan.
> (64–70)

This piece of play acting discloses that gender is unstable, because sexual identities are bound up with processes of representation. Only two spots, and nothing more, separate the male from the female swan. Similarly, only facial hair draws a distinction between men and women. But these gamish memories cannot overcome his sense of loss. The nature of their row is never revealed but it completely broke their ideal union. He implores her: 'Woman, and will you cast/For a word, quite off at last, /Me, your own, your You' (92–5), adding 'I was You all the happy past' (96). In every stanza, he attempts to recreate, and tries to comprehend, how and why they made images of one another, relished their time together, and then quarrelled. For this there is no answer. All he can do is wait for her to come back to him at 'twelve o' clock' (150) when 'In the worst of a storm's uproar, /I shall pull her through the door' (152–3). Intent on possessing her entirely, he finally declares: 'I shall have her for evermore!' (154). He now seems to want to take their games seriously. Perhaps she will suffer the same fate as Porphyria who similarly seeks comfort from the stormy world outside?

One of the lover's memories refers to the immediate political context in which Browning produced most of *Men and Women*. The speaker recalls reading in *The Times* an announcement of Napoleon III's marriage: 'He has taken a bride/To his gruesome side' (31–2). The Brownings spent much of the late 1840s and early 1850s in Paris, and they followed closely the events that led up to Napoleon III's *coup d'état* in 1851. Browning found it hard to reconcile himself to this sudden act, since it brought to an abrupt halt to what little hope of democracy there was left in France. One poem, in particular, strikes at the double standards that operate in so many levels of society, both political and personal, and this is 'Respectability'. Browning's speaker refers to the induction of the ultramontane Comte de Montalembert into the Académie Française in 1852. As leader of the clerical party, Montalembert was a powerful figure. Since 1848 he had been seeking Napoleon III's support for the church's control of education. He embodied values entirely anathema to Browning. His entry into the French Institute was marked by a rapid switch of political loyalties. For in 1852 he had lost faith the emperor for making grants-in-aid out of the capital raised on the Orléanist properties, rather than giving the money to the church. Browning attended the Académie to observe whether some of Montalembert's enemies, such as François Guizot, would see fit to applaud this man. At what price respectability? When and how should codes of honour be upheld? These are the questions at the centre of the poem. But its field of reference extends beyond the French academy.

Here, an 'unrespectable' woman acknowledges how her chosen way of life challenges bourgeois mores. Roy E. Gridley observes that she resembles George Sand – the 'large-brained woman and large-hearted man' who filled Barrett Browning with so much admiration in 'A Desire' (from *Poems* (1844)).[13] Sand was the only woman writer in France to have achieved an eminence comparable to any of her male peers, and she stood as a prominent member of the liberal opposition to Napoleon III. Both Brownings were eager to meet her, and this they achieved in February 1852. They were courteously received. Sand's lifestyle was controversial; she lived, out of wedlock, with her lover. Given his respect for Sand's accomplishments, Browning recognised the compromises she was obliged to make in forging a career as an independent woman in a man's world. So great was her influence on Barrett Browning, it has been suggested that Aurora Leigh was modelled on Sand, but not without first being purged of any taint of immorality.[14] In 'Respectability', the woman tells the man she loves that she must disguise her affection for him, lest society becomes so intolerant they will not be able to be seen anywhere in public. The whole poem reads:

> Dear, had the world in its caprice
>> Deigned to proclaim 'I know you both,
>> Have recognized your plighted troth,
> Am sponsor for you: live in peace!' –
> How many precious months and years   5
>> Of youth had passed, that speed so fast,
>> Before we found it out at last,
> The world, and what it fears?
>
> How much of priceless life were spent
>> With men that every virtue decks,   10
>> And women models of their sex,
> Society's true ornament, –
> Ere we dared wander, nights like this,
>> Through wind and rain, and watch the Seine,
>> And feel the Boulevart break again   15
> To warmth and light and bliss?
>
> I know! the world proscribes not love;
>> Allows my finger to caress
>> Your lips' contour and downiness,
> Provided it supply a glove.   20
> The world's good word! – the Institute!
>> Guizot receives Montalembert!
>> Eh? down the court three lampions flare:
> Put forward your best foot!

The hypocrisy she decries is all too clear to see. Women can only be respectable as long as they serve as 'models of their sex', and that means remaining decorative, passive and unthinking. This was the feminine ideal enshrined in Coventry Patmore's *The Angel in the House* (the first book of this epic was published in 1854), and here it has to be rejected. A woman may, it appears, only be a man's equal outside marriage, if under the most ridiculous constraints: the woman knows she can only touch his face with a gloved hand, anything else would be improper. Propriety creates all sorts of obstacles, not just in women's, but all human lives. At a time of political instability, 'the world's good word' is thoroughly corrupting. But she will not be overcome. She tells her lover they must not lose faith in themselves, and so, presumably, they go arm in arm through the city, ignoring the querulous goings on at the academy. Not all of Browning's female lovers in *Men and Women* are as forthright and defiant.

One poem, 'A Woman's Last Word', reveals the appalling concessions women have to make to their husbands. Here, marriage subsists on wholly patriarchal terms. The discontented woman finds herself too frightened to tell her husband how unhappy she is with him and the authority he exercises over every aspect of her life. Turning over her thoughts as she lies next to him, she realises that she must never tempt fate; she knows only too well the precedent before her: 'Where the apple reddens/Never pry –/Lest we lose our Edens,/Eve and I' (17–20). Mentally pleading with him to fulfil his conventional role –' Be a god and hold me/With a charm' (21–2) – she is resigned to 'bury' her 'sorrow/Out of sight' (35–6). In her first collection of highly popular *Legends and Lyrics* (1858), Adelaide Anne Procter adopted the form and title of Browning's poem in an act of startling revision.[15] Her woman's last word is strongly assertive: 'So I tell you plainly/It must be:/I shall try, not vainly,/To be free'. Only later, in 'James Lee's Wife' (1864) would Browning reach a similarly feminist position from which he could activate a woman's voice to contest men's abuse of power in marriage.

Men and Women, in the handful of poems with female speakers, is at times underconfident about a woman's capability to break emotional ties with men. The seemingly ailing woman of 'Any Wife to Any Husband' sounds an equivocal tone, caught, on the verge of death, between wanting to hold on to an ideal of eternal love, and knowing that the husband she is leaving is likely to be disloyal to her memory. Although she believes her husband to be 'all truth' (2), and that their love is God given (God 'never is dishonoured in the spark/He gave us from his fire of fires' (21)), her anxiety lies in what shall happen after she has passed into the grave. Will he say, '"she is immortally my bride;/Chance cannot change my love"' (53–4)? Is it right and proper for him to turn his affections to another woman? Her mood switches rapidly in the ensuing stanzas. Love, if a divine gift, also involves so many sacrifices that she feels robbed of her integrity:

> So I must see, from where I sit and watch
> My own self sell myself, my hand attach
>   Its warrant to the very thefts from me –
> Thy singleness of soul that made me proud,
> Thy purity of heart I loved aloud,
>   Thy man's-truth I was bold to bid God see!
>
> Love so then, if thou wilt! Give all thou canst
> Away to the new faces – disentranced,
>   (Say it and think it) obdurate no more:
> Re-issue looks and words from the old mint,
> Pass them afresh, no matter whose the print
>   Image and superscription once they bore!
>   (79–90)

Working through this suggestive monetary metaphor, she feels that she has prostituted herself to him. She gives her love; he thrives on it; and then, once she is dead, he may profit. But, she hesitates, is this wrong? Perhaps he must 'Re-issue' himself? Because, perhaps, he seeks further 'issue'. The pun is intentional. For here the Victorian 'spermatic economy' is surely in circulation. Men, inevitably, must 'Re-coin' (91) themselves. Recognising that she has hoarded up a whole 'treasure' (95) from him, she knows it would be selfish were he not able to 'spend' (91) himself on other women. He cannot be consigned to a life of celibacy. Yet the thought of it still discomforts her. At the very end of the poem, she imagines dying in his arms until she will 'wake saved' in heaven, and yet has to add 'it will not be!' (126). Under such circumstances, fidelity remains an impossibility. She cannot resolve whether this is a physical or ethical matter.

One point, however, which is obvious is her questioning approach to sexual desire – it is in conflict with the structures of the marriage vow. Eternal faithfulness is certainly too much to ask of any partner in love. The poem which opens *Dramatis Personae* scrutinises a middle-class woman's uneasy thoughts on marriage more closely than perhaps anywhere else in his work. Given the woman's profound equivocations of feeling, it should come as no surprise that Browning worried over the title of this nine-part sequence of lyrics. Originally published as 'James Lee', it was retitled as 'James Lee's Wife' in the *Poetical Works* of 1868 (the poem was also heavily revised). Significantly shifting the emphasis from the identity of the speaker's desire to that of speaker herself, the new title obviously focuses on the fact that she is her husband's property, a point to which she returns on many occasions:

> And such as you were, I took you for mine:
>   Did not you find me yours,
> To watch the olive and wait the vine,
> And wonder when the rivers of oil and wine
>   Would flow, as the Book assures?
>   (102–6)

James Lee's wife would appear to be invoking verses from Deuteronomy (8: 7–10) where the Israelites are told of the promised land. Although 'love greatens and glories, / Till God's a-glow, to the loving eyes, / In what was mere earth before' (89–91), the 'earth' from which God-given love grows is also where it perishes. A mere mortal, James Lee is understandably 'weak earth', where 'plenty of passions' have 'run to seed' (99–100), reminding us of the landscapes depicted in 'Two in the Campagna' and 'Love among the Ruins'. But these words are not scornful. In fact, the tone of the poem is not one of embittered personal betrayal. Rather, the woman attempts to rationalise the man's waywardness: 'I will be quiet and talk with you, / And reason why you are wrong' (81–3). Unreproachful, she knows that there is in him 'a little good grain too' (101). The tone is altogether fair-minded, neither compliant nor aggressive.

Although James Lee's wife sees their plight as an 'old story', she reckons her 'despair' is a 'Fit subject for some new song' (115–16) – which is precisely the nature of this largely elegiac and meditative sequence. Her 'new song' is a highly innovative examination of the 'open hell' (52) that may lurk beneath the voyage undertaken by two young people in marriage, and which Victorian respectability desperately sought to conceal. Browning seemed not entirely happy with his achievement. In one of his letters to Julia Wedgwood (a correspondence that collapsed after his own amorous advances towards this young and powerfully intellectual young woman were repelled), he remarked:

> I misled you into thinking the couple were 'prolétaire' – but I meant them for just the opposite – people newly-married, trying to realize a dream of being sufficient to each other, in a foreign land (where you can try such an experiment) and finding it break up, – the man being tired *first*, and tired precisely because of the love: – but I have expressed it all insufficiently.[16]

These comments show how he was trying to imagine marriage in an entirely unanticipated context – where each partner could enjoy a measure of independence while remaining 'sufficient' to one another. (Perhaps Wedgwood imagined such a relationship was only possible among the working class?) Brittany, rather than Britain, provides the setting so that Mr and Mrs Lee may experience love not only *in* but also *as* a foreign country. Although the poem does not imply the exact context suggested by Browning's letter, it may be thought that the greater freedom afforded by their time in Brittany was more than the husband could endure.

The wife can see only too well that the institution of marriage makes unreasonable demands on individuals. It wrongly leads them to believe that love will last forever. At least, that is its premise. By definition, the world is endlessly mutable, and this, she argues, is surely part of God's design:

Nothing can be as it has been before;
  Better, so call it, only not the same.
To draw one beauty into our hearts' core,
  And keep it changeless! such our claim;
So answered, – Never more!

Simple? Why this is the old woe o' the world;
  Tune, to whose rise and fall we live and die.
Rise with it, then! Rejoice that man is hurled
  From change to change unceasingly,
His soul's wings never furled!

That's a new question; still replies the fact,
  Nothing endures: the wind moans, saying so;
We moan in acquiescence: there's life's pact,
  Perhaps probation – do *I* know?
God does: endure his act!
                    (212–26)

Each stanza advances its points by keeping a completely open mind to unforeseen possibilities. Change must be accepted. Recognising the vicissitudes of human relations, her resilient line of thinking – modulating between rhetorical pleas, statements of affirmation and exclamations – eventually prompts a 'new' and important 'question'; she comes to understand that there can be no resolution to the mutability of this world since it has been put into restless play by God. That, all in all, is 'life's pact', and she is now reconciled to it.

The longest section of the poem takes the mood of the poem in a different direction – towards deeper self-discovery. James Lee's wife does not allow herself to remain dejected. Instead, she chooses to act upon her situation. To do so, she turns to art. For art offers the hope of some kind of emotional redemption. But she has to learn that she is in error if she thinks art may act as a substitute for the love she has lost. In the exceptionally complex seventh section, 'Beside the Drawing-Board', she sketches the clay cast of a young working girl's hand. She wants to copy it perfectly. As she ponders the close resemblances between her own hand and the cast she is drawing, one phrase preys on her mind: '"As like a Hand to another Hand"' (244, 253). These words linger with her because they form a startling connection. They focus on a haunting and disturbing pun. Hands, capitalised like this, allude to workers, as well as individual plaster moulds. To some members of the bourgeoisie, one Hand was indistinguishable from another. Hands simply comprised the masses, as this synecdochic form of reference makes demeaningly clear. Dickens emphasised this point in *Hard Times* (1854) where the narrator refers to 'the multitude of Coketown [an imaginary town in the North of England], generically "the Hands", – a race who would have found more favour with some people, if Providence had seen fit to make them only hands'.[17] Such a class-bound attitude, she thinks, is 'foolish' (245). For by studying this 'Little girl with the poor coarse hand' (292), she recognises the beauty of the human body, which no class distinctions may corrupt. And, moreover, she is struck by the similarities between herself and the peasant girl; this 'Hand' was also married. 'Princess-like', she, too, 'wears the ring' (272).

The wedding ring had been placed there by an artist. We

may assume that this peasant woman had served as his model, and that he, in the course of his work, finally fell in love with her. Although he was a 'soaring genius' (276), he surely understood, as James Lee's wife understands, that no drawing could ever 'Mend the lines and make them true' (298). Earthly art is unable to capture such heavenly beauty. As any practised artist will concur, it may take years before a mere mortal may reproduce a human image exactly. She imagines Leonardo da Vinci reproving her for her naivety: '"Shall earth and the cramped moment-space/Yield the heavenly crowning grace?"' (320–1). He, like the voice of conscience, states that she cannot continue in life complaining '"I must live beloved or die!"' (316). Life goes on, and the world changes. A peasant girl cannot be beautiful forever, since she 'spins the wool/And bakes the bread' (327–8). The clay cast shows something exquisite – but which, in real life, would have grown calloused. In asking, finally, '"What use survives the beauty?"' (330), the voice of Leonardo is informing James Lee's wife that perfection is not to be possessed in this world. The purpose of art, in its partial revelation of God, is to remind human beings that there is no eternity on earth, only glimpses of what is to come. Having heard the master speak, she declares: 'I have learned my lesson, shall understand' (332). Thereafter, she can 'set' James Lee 'free' (337) from the mind and body he attempted to own. For him, their love was one-sided; he took all the initiatives: 'A tenure of breath at your lips' decree,/A Passion to stand as your thoughts approve, A rapture to fall where your foot might be' (360–2). Now she can live on her own terms, and, legally, it was for the first time possible to do so. The Divorce Act of 1857 gave power to the courts to break up the marriage vow. Formerly, divorces had only been accessible to the rich, since each and every one had to pass through its own act of parliament.

After *Dramatic Personae*, Browning set to work on *The Ring and the Book*. This vastly ambitious poem tells the story of the most horrible marriage imaginable. Based on the intricate legal proceedings of a murder trial that occurred in Rome in 1698 (the 'Old Yellow Book' that Browning found on a market stall), all twelve books of this epic gave voice to different characters who provide their own versions and opinions of how and why an ageing aristocrat, Guido Francheschini, came to marry and then avenge his much younger bride, Pompilia Comparini, and her parents. The plot is thickened by layers of deceit. Guido made an attempt on her life because of her involvement with Giuseppe Caponsacchi, a young priest, who risks his reputation by trying to rescue Pompilia from the brutal Guido. For Pompilia has been raped, battered and abused in the course of marriage because she has not brought the dowry Guido had expected. In fact, he discovers that her mother bought her from a prostitute. Violante Comparini had her own reasons for doing so. The Comparini were a respectable middle-class couple. But they were short of money. Unable to bear children, Violante realised that their financial state would worsen if there were no son-in-law in place to relieve them of their debts in old age. Deceiving her husband, Pietro, she bought Pompilia, and the Comparini raised her to believe she was their own child. At the age of twelve, they circulated the news that she was prepared for marriage, with a large dowry. This proved attractive to Guido, who, at fifty, was poor, unmarried, with an unsuccessful career on the margins of the priesthood (he had not taken final vows). Pompilia seemed an excellent bargain. She would bring him wealth, sexual pleasure and a son to continue the noble Francheschini line. Once more, Violante took it upon herself to deceive her husband, and carried Pompilia off to church to have her married in secret. It was a further foolish act that would contribute to an appalling tragedy. At this time, Guido, of course, had no knowledge of Pompilia's true origins, and that he had been defrauded by the Comparini.

Once married, Pompilia was settled into Guido's house at Arezzo. Her parents, now having parted with their money, were obliged to accompany them. Everyone was unhappy. It would seem that Guido was, from the outset, behaving tyrannically. Matters worsened when Violante, now suffering from an aching conscience, decided to confess her sin to the authorities. Pompilia's illegitimate status was discovered, and Pietro Comparini, after the case had been heard at court, repudiated his daughter. Both Pompilia's parents and Guido spurned her, and Guido required some evidence upon which he could rightly dispose of her. In the meantime, Pompilia looked to the church authorities for safety. No one would help, given the powerful influence the Francheschini family held over the church at Arezzo. It was only when Caponsacchi heard of her plight, and saw the sheer injustice of it, that she felt there was some future for herself and, more pressingly, her unborn child. Caponsacchi engineered her escape. But Guido chased after them, and charges were laid against this ostensibly dishonour-able pair – a young adulteress and a disreputable priest. Yet Guido was not satisfied. He wanted a divorce. However, on hearing of Pompilia's pregnancy, he decided to kill all the Comparini. Pompilia lived for four days after sustaining twenty-two stabs wounds, five of them lethal. Her monologue, which occupies Book VII of the poem, takes places during this brief period. Telling her story to the friar Don Celestine, she reveals herself, at the age of seventeen, as anything but a passive victim of the cruel events that have occurred. Bold, upstanding, honest and intellectually acute, Pompilia embod-ies the female will at its most resistant. As Brady observes:

> Pompilia Comparini, who comes across the pages of the Old Yellow Book as an unfortunate, faceless victim, Browning has transformed into a brave, self-directed young woman. Chained by the helplessness society devised for wives, she seeks help from that society and finds none. Ultimately she finds her rescuer outside the structures. Pompilia flees her husband with the aid of a priest who, by all expectations, should have urged her to remain and accept 'the proper lot of women' [as in the teachings of St Paul, St

Augustine and St Thomas Aquinas]. She loves Caponsacchi without desiring physical consummation – loves in a way that culturally redefines *love* as *caritas*. On her deathbed, she divorces and unfathers her husband because of the crimes he has committed against her. And, simultaneously with these clear-sighted and tough-minded judgments, Pompilia forgives her rapist-murderer.[18]

This is an important, and for perhaps the first time, accurate summary of Pompilia's extraordinary resistance to the most severe abuse of patriarchal authority. Earlier criticism had characterised her as 'the antithesis to the fallen Eve'.[19] And there was a tendency to view *The Ring and the Book* as a symmetrically perfect battle between her good against Guido's evil. Browning's world was never so neatly divided. For Guido, horrific as his actions are, has also been badly misled. Pompilia can knows that he, too, has fallen prey to her mother's actions: 'is it not true/He was ill-used and cheated of his hope/To get enriched by marriage?' (VII. 638–40). But this does not mean (and here I would dissent from Brady's point) that Pompilia can 'forgive' Guido. For he has committed marital rape. Rather, Pompilia finally comprehends the circumstances that have led him to perpetrate such dreadful crimes. Pompilia's speech returns to Guido's sexual violence on several occasions. Only on her death-bed has she come to understand what she was supposed to mean to him as a wife:

> Now I have got to die and see thing clear.
> Remember I was barely twelve years old –
> A child at marriage: I was let alone
> For weeks, I told you, lived my child-life still
> Even at Arezzo, when I woke and found
> First . . . but I need not think of that again –
> Over and ended! Try and take the sense
> Of what I signify, if it must be so.
> After the first, my husband, for hate's sake,
> Said one eve, when the simpler cruelty

Seemed somewhat dull at edge and fit to bear,
'We have been man and wife six months almost:
How long is this your comedy to last?
Go this night to my chamber, not your own!'
(VII. 733–46)

So much of *The Ring and the Book* is given over to the
question of marriage as an exclusively, and dangerously,
contractual relation that it becomes difficult to think of any
true, pure and spiritual love occurring within its restrictive
bounds. Pompilia, at first, would prefer to be a nun than suffer
at the hands of Guido. But in Caponsacchi, she discovers that
love need not be sexual. He does not desire her body but
communes with her soul. Just as she has learned to comprehend
what she might 'signify' – as a daughter, wife, mother, and,
most important of all, individual in this world – so too has
Caponsacchi learned to 'read' her 'mark':

I did think, do think, in the thought shall die,
That to have Caponsacchi for my guide,
Ever the face upturned to mine, the hand
Holding my hand across the world, – a sense
That reads, as only such can read, the mark
God sets on woman, signifying so
She should – shall peradventure – be divine;
Yet 'ware, the while, how weakness mars the print
And makes confusion, leaves the thing men see,
– Not this man, – who from his own soul, re-writes
The obliterated charter, – love and strength
Mending what's marred.
(VII. 1494–1506)

Pompilia, herself illiterate, knows only too clearly the power
invested in reading and writing. Her apprehension of literacy –
the encoding and decoding of signs – has extraordinary
resonance here. For she, as a woman, is the most vulnerable
sign to circulate in a signifying economy dominated by men.

Not only does her understanding of 'signifying' suggest that true love depends upon the finest skills of interpretation, it also implies that poetry – the highly literate art in which these words are framed – has the ability to make amends for the limitations of the written code, and thereby indicate that there is something 'divine' even in words where 'weakness mars the print'. The metaphor expects to be extended in this way because, from the start, *The Ring and the Book* is fascinated with the semantic properties of the overarching ring metaphor introduced and elaborated in the first book: ''Tis a figure, a symbol, say;/A thing's sign: now for the thing signified' (I. 31–2). Pompilia's speech reveals processes of self-signification. She has reached a point in her life where she can see what she has meant to the contending parties around her, and how Caponsacchi was the only person not to misrepresent or misread her.

But her words, finally, disclose one of the main antagonisms in Browning's writing on gender. Although Pompilia's integrity is never in question, her speech, if designed to sound modest, bears the traces of those of a Victorian man not quite sure about the female subjectivity he has created. These lines are, admittedly, extremely compacted. Yet it is where Browning's syntax is at its most awkward that it may begin to disclose his greatest uncertainties. There is surely a problem here in interpreting the word 'weakness'. Does female 'weakness' mar the 'print'? Or is it men's 'weakness' that fails to read 'the mark/God sets on women'? Who or what is responsible? All that is left is 'confusion'. Even if it is a commonplace since Freud to speak of the enigma of 'woman', femininity in Browning's poetry remains a difficult book to put down. 'Pompilia' is some measure of his own attempt – like Caponsacchi's – to recover the 'obliterated charter' (women's rights) and let her speak out. And yet the 'mark' of woman – as her puzzling 'sign' – remains.

Two years before he started thinking about a five-act drama against women's suffrage, Browning included in *Jocoseria* (1883) a poem about Mary Wollstonecraft, author of *Vindication*

of the Rights of Woman (1792). He had been led to believe
that Wollstonecraft sustained an unrequited love for the artist,
Henry Fuseli (there was, in fact, no truth in this). Here is how
he represents the voice of the eminent feminist theorist whose
works he would have surely known from his earliest acquaintance with the *Monthly Repository*:

> Oh but is it not hard, Dear?
>   Mine are the nerves to quake at a mouse:
> If a spider drops I shrink with fear:
>   I should die outright in a haunted house;
> While for you – did the danger dared bring help –
> From a lion's den I could steal his whelp,
> With a serpent round me, stand stock-still,
> Go sleep in a churchyard, – so would will
> Give me the power to dare and do
> Valiantly – just for you!
>
> (1–10)

Although Browning permits Wollstonecraft to speak of her
considerable intellectual and artistic capabilities ('I toil at a
language, tax my brain/Attempting to draw' (12–13)), she is
revealed as a typical bourgeois lady, who is scared of mice, and
frightened of spiders, and who needs, above all, a man to
support her. For love, it seems, she would sacrifice anything,
including her own life. Sexual longing consumes her will – and
for nothing. There is no reward or 'due' for 'the strong fierce
heart's love's labour' (29). Her reputation was certainly not
based upon this trivialising image. Why should Wollstonecraft
be remembered in this way? Is it supposed to be as patronising
as it sounds? Or is it making a rather different point about
the conflict between the woman intellectual's mind and her
sexuality? There are no clear answers to these questions. They
only serve to indicate Browning's fascination with assertive
femininity and how this stood in opposition to his sense of the
natural weakness of the female sex. In other words, here he is

trying to imagine Wollstonecraft as a kind of Andromeda waiting to be saved. Except this time there is no Perseus. Perhaps that is the penalty for the woman who seeks to assert her rights? And possibly that is why Browning felt so uneasy about women obtaining the vote?

In his longest, and most complex, poem on sexuality, *Fifine at the Fair* (1872), Browning creates a Victorian Don Juan who compares and contrasts his liking for two opposed feminine types – his wife, the respectable Elvire, and Fifine, a circus performer. They excite conflicting desires within him. But they share one quality that prompts his infuriated response: 'Few families were racked/By torture self-supplied, did Nature grant but this –/That women comprehend mental analysis!' (508–11). Maybe such outrageous misogyny should only be expected of such a notorious character, drawn from Molière's play of 1665, and Byron's poem of 1819? But the fact that Browning adapted this figure, and allowed him to utter such sentiments, compares just as unfavourably with the voice he lends to Wollstonecraft. Yet where they may seem poles apart, they both express a surging, fiery desire that flames within them. Browning never seems able to understand relations between this God-given gift (Pompilia calls it a 'power') and the cultural work of gender. No doubt he was fortunate to base his aesthetic on an enduring scepticism. As Don Juan says: 'Words struggle with the weight/So feebly of the False, thick element between /Our soul, the True, the Truth' (943–5). Until old age, Browning knew only too well that he could not know why God had made the world as it was. But the divine rationale that placed a gendered 'mark' between men and women appears to have baffled him more than anything else. It was his greatest negativity – the one thing he tried most strenuously of all to 'read'.

Notes

Preface

1. Herbert F. Tucker Jr., *Browning's Beginnings: The Art of Disclosure* (Minneapolis, MN: University of Minnesota Press, 1980), p. 3.
2. Richard D. Altick, 'Introduction' to *The Ring and the Book* (Harmondsworth: Penguin Books, 1971), p. 13.

Chapter 1

1. E.F. Benson, *As We Were: A Victorian Peep-Show* (1930; London: The Hogarth Press, 1985), pp. 143–4. Austin Dobson (1840–1921) was a minor poet, known best for his light verse.
2. Oscar Wilde, 'The Critic as Artist' (1890, 1891) in J.B. Foreman, ed., *Complete Works of Oscar Wilde* (London: Collins, 1966), pp. 1012–13. George Meredith (1828–1909), poet and novelist, counts among the more stylistically difficult Victorian writers. His work, too, anticipates Modernist techniques.
3. For a helpful analysis of the connections between the aesthetic choices of Victorian poets and their Modernist successors, see Carol T. Christ, *Victorian and Modern Poetics* (Chicago, IL: University of Chicago Press, 1984). Christ discusses Pound's responses to Browning on pp. 120–7.
4. 'An Essay on the Poetic Character of Percy Bysshe Shelley, and on the Probable Tendency of His Writings', *Metropolitan Quarterly Review*, 2 (1826), p. 191. In 1828 another reviewer was led to write: 'Since the death of Byron, there has been no King in Israel': Review of Edwin Atherstone, *The Fall of Nineveh, a Poem*, *Edinburgh Review*, 48 (1828), p. 47; and several years later, the feeling was much the same: 'In the department of poetry we have had nothing for several years worth mentioning': 'C.H.', 'Literature in 1834', *New Monthly Magazine*, 40 (1834), p. 498.

NOTES

5. All quotations from Wordsworth's poetry are taken from *Poetical Works*, eds. Thomas Hutchinson and Ernest de Selincourt (London: Oxford University Press, 1936).
6. Thomas Carlyle, *On Heroes, Hero-Worship, and the Heroic in History*, *The Works of Thomas Carlyle in Thirty Volumes*, Centenary Edition (1841; London: Chapman and Hall, 1901), V.
7. John Ruskin, 'To Robert Browning', 2 December 1855, in David J. DeLaura, 'Ruskin and the Brownings: twenty-five unpublished letters', *Bulletin of the John Rylands Library*, 54 (1972), p. 324.
8. Browning, 'To John Ruskin', 10 December 1855, E. T. Cook and Alexander Wedderburn, eds., *The Works of John Ruskin*, 38 vols (London: Allen, 1903–9), XXXVI, p. xxxiv.
9. The preface to the 1835 edition of *Paracelsus* is not reprinted in the Penguin edition. See Ian Jack, ed., *Browning: Poetical Works, 1833–1864* (London: Oxford University Press, 1970), p. 38.
10. 'Introductory essay', John Pettigrew and Thomas J. Collins, eds., *The Poems*, 2 vols (London: Penguin, 1981), I, p. 1002. All further page references are included in the text.
11. Harold Bloom's psycho-poetics devises a system of tropes largely drawn from Freud: see *The Anxiety of Influence: A Theory of Poetry* (New York: Oxford University Press, 1973); *A Map of Misreading* (New York: Oxford University Press, 1975), especially pp. 106–22; and 'Introduction: reading Browning', in Bloom and Adrienne Munich, eds., *Robert Browning: A Collection of Critical Essays* (Englewood Cliffs, NJ: Prentice Hall, 1979), pp. 1–12.
12. On 11 October 1881 Hopkins wrote to Richard Watson Dixon: 'He [Browning] has got a great deal of what came in with Kingsley and the Broad Church School [those in favour of a more liberal church], a way of talking (and making his people talk) with the air and spirit of a man bouncing up from table with his mouth full of bread and cheese saying that he meant to stand no blasted nonsense': *The Correspondence of Gerard Manley Hopkins and Richard Watson Dixon*, ed. Claude Colleer Abbott (London: Oxford University Press, 1935), p. 74. Hopkins, a Roman Catholic convert, with strong High Church sympathies, was drawn from a middle-class faction very different from Browning's.
13. Herbert F. Tucker Jr., *Browning's Beginnings: The Art of Disclosure* (Minneapolis, MN: University of Minnesota Press, 1980), p. 5.
14. C.S. Calverley, *The Complete Works* (London: George Bell, 1902), pp. 111–12.
15. Walter Bagehot's essay, 'Wordsworth, Tennyson and Browning; or Pure, Ornate, and Grotesque Art in English Poetry', appeared in the *National Review*, 19 (1864), pp. 27–57. In his unsympathetic essay, 'The Poetry of Barbarism' (1900), Santayana writes: 'Apart from a certain superficial grotesqueness to which we are soon accustomed, he easily arouses and engages the reader by the pithiness of his phrase, the volume of his passion, the vigour of his moral judgement, the liveliness of his historical fancy. It is obvious that we are in the presence of a great writer, of a great imaginative force, of a master in the expression of emotion. What is perhaps not so obvious, but no less true, is that we are in the presence of a barbaric genius, of a truncated imagination, of a thought and an art inchoate and ill-digested, of a volcanic eruption that tosses itself quite blindly and ineffectually into the sky': Boyd Litzinger and K. L. Knickerbocker, eds., *The Browning Critics* (Lexington, KT: University of Kentucky Press, 1965), p. 57.
16. Alfred Austin, *The Poetry of the Period* (London: Strahan, 1870), p. 64.

17. Isobel Armstrong, 'Browning and the "Grotesque" style', in Isobel Armstrong, ed., *The Major Victorian Poets: Reconsiderations* (London: Routledge and Kegan Paul, 1969), p. 93.
18. Bloom, 'Introduction: reading Browning', p. 1, op. cit.

Chapter 2

1. [George Eliot], Review of *Men and Women*, *Westminster Review*, 65 (1856), pp. 290–6, reprinted in Boyd Litzinger and Donald Smalley, eds., *Browning: The Critical Heritage* (London: Routledge and Kegan Paul, 1970), p. 174.
2. Ibid., pp. 174–5.
3. *Poetical Works, 1833–1864*, ed. Ian Jack (London: Oxford University Press, 1970), p. 38.
4. Browning, 'To André Victor Amédée de Ripert-Monclar', 2 March 1835, *The Brownings' Correspondence*, eds. Philip Kelley and Ronald Hudson (Winfield, KA: Wedgestone Press, 1985), III, pp. 126–7.
5. Browning, 'To Richard Henry [Hengist] Horne', 3 December 1848, *Letters of Robert Browning Collected by Thomas J Wise*, ed. Thurman L. Hood (New Haven, CT: Yale University Press, 1933), p. 20.
6. Browning, 'To Euphrasia Fanny Haworth', April 1839, *New Letters of Robert Browning*, eds. William Clyde DeVane and K. L. Knickerbocker (New Haven, CT: Yale University Press, 1950), p. 17.
7. [W. J. Fox], Review of *Pauline; a Fragment of a Confession*, *Monthly Repository*, NS 77 (1833), pp. 252–62; Review of *Paracelsus*, NS 9 (1835), pp. 716–27. Five poems by Browning appeared in Fox's journal: 'Sonnet', NS 8 (1834), p. 712; 'The King' (later included in *Pippa Passes* (1841)), NS 9 (1835), pp. 707–8; 'Porphyria' (later entitled 'Porphyria's Lover' and placed, under the heading 'Madhouse Cells' with 'Johannes Agricola' in *Dramatic Lyrics* (1842)), NS 10 (1836), pp. 43–4; 'Johannes Agricola' (later entitled 'Johannes Agricola in Meditation'), NS 10 (1836), pp. 45–6; 'Lines' (later included in 'James Lee', *Dramatis Personae* (1834), later entitled 'James Lee's Wife' in 1868), NS 10 (1836), pp. 270–1. Browning's attachment to Fox is explored in Richard Garnett, *The Life of W. J. Fox: Public Teacher and Social Reformer, 1786–1864* (London: John Lane, The Bodley Head, 1910), especially pp. 312–23; the involvement of both men in the *Monthly Repository* is detailed in Francis E. Mineka, *The Dissidence of Dissent: The Monthly Repository, 1806–1838, Under the Editorship of Robert Aspland, W. J. Fox, R. H. Horne, and Leigh Hunt* (Chapel Hill, NC: University of North Carolina Press, 1944). See also C. R. Tracy, 'Browning's Heresies', *Studies in Philology*, 33 (1936), pp. 610–25. Additional information of the Fox circle is to be found in Ann Blainey, *The Farthing Poet: A Biography of Richard Hengist Horne 1902–84: A Lesser Literary Lion* (London: Longmans, 1968), pp. 57–69. Two poems from the early collection by Browning that Fox passed judgement on, 'Incondita', are reprinted the Penguin edition of *The Poems*, II, pp. 935–40.
8. Browning wrote to Ripert-Monclar in December 1834: 'did my long answer [to your last letter] strike terror into the stout heart that all Bentham's big Books could never appal? . . . I shall triumph not a little in the fallibility of my grand model and proposed exemplar of constancy[,] precision, punctuality etc, etc': *The Brownings' Correspondence*, III, p. 107. Here, Browning is referring to moral qualities listed in Bentham's *Deontology* (1819–20). As John Maynard notes in his biography of the young Browning, the poet introduces Bentham into his letter

because Ripart-Monclar (like many French intellectuals at the time) was fascinated by Utilitarianism. It is, however, surprising to read Maynard's claim that Bentham is 'a writer of whom one would otherwise suppose Browning had never heard': *Browning's Youth* (Cambridge, MA: Harvard University Press, 1977), p. 126.

9. The phrase was taken from Priestley's *Essay on Government* (1768). Leslie Stephen shows that this Utilitarian slogan has an earlier source, among several others, in Francis Hutcheson's *Enquiry Concerning Moral Good and Evil* (1725): *The English Utilitarians*, Society of Reprints of Scarce Works on Political Economy No. 9, 3 vols (London: The London School of Economics and Political Science, 1950), I, p. 178.

10. Isobel Armstrong, 'Arnoldian repressions: two forgotten discourses of culture', *News from Nowhere*, 5 (1988), p. 41.

11. Jeremy Bentham, *The Works of Jeremy Bentham*, ed. John Bowring (London: William Tait, 1843), II, p. 213 cited in F. Parvin Sharpless, *The Literary Criticism of John Stuart Mill* (The Hague: Mouton, 1967), p. 32. Sharpless's study contains a useful discussion of Utilitarianism and poetry: see pp. 24–32.

12. Jeremy Bentham, *The Rationale of Reward* in *The Works of Jeremy Bentham*, II, p. 253.

13. Jeremy Bentham, *Deontology together with A Table of the Springs of Action and the Article on Utilitarianism*, ed. Amnon Goldworth (Oxford: Clarendon Press, 1985), p. 90.

14. [Peregrine Bingham], Review of Thomas Moore, *Fables of Holy Alliance*, *Westminster Review*, 1 (1824), p. 19.

15. [W. J. Fox], 'Coleridge and Poetry', *Westminster Review*, 12 (1830), p. 3.

16. [W. J. Fox], Review of Alfred Tennyson, *Poems, Chiefly Lyrical*, *Westminster Review*, 14 (1831), pp. 210–24, reprinted in Isobel Armstrong, *Victorian Scrutinies: Reviews of Poetry 1830–1870* (London: Athlone Press, 1972), p. 76. Relations between Fox's interest in 'mental states' and wider developments in the Victorian monologue are detailed in Ekbert Faas, *Retreat into the Mind: Victorian Poetry and the Rise of Psychiatry* (Princeton, NJ: Princeton University Press, 1988); see, in particular, pp. 19–83.

17. [W. J. Fox], Review of *Poems, Chiefly Lyrical* in *Victorian Scrutinies*, p. 83.

18. John Stuart Mill, *Autobiography*, ed. Jack Stillinger (London: Oxford University Press, 1971), pp. 86, 89.

19. John Stuart Mill, 'Thoughts on Poetry and Its Varieties' (1857) in *Autobiography and Literary Essays*, eds. John M. Robson and Jack Stillinger (Toronto: University of Toronto Press, 1981), p. 344. All references to this essay are included in the text. 'Thoughts on Poetry and Its Varieties' is a revised version of the two essays on poetry Mill published in the *Monthly Repository* in 1833.

20. William Wordsworth, 'Preface' to *Lyrical Ballads* (1800, 1802), eds. R. L. Brett and A. R. Jones (London: Methuen, 1965), p. 246.

21. M. H. Abrams, *The Mirror and the Lamp: Romantic Theory and the Critical Tradition* (New York: Oxford University Press, 1953), p. 25.

22. [T. H. Lister], Review of *Philip Van Artevelde: A Dramatic Romance* by Henry Taylor, *Edinburgh Review*, 60 (1835), pp. 7, 4–5.

23. Herbert F. Tucker Jr., *Browning's Beginnings: The Art of Disclosure* (Minneapolis, MN: University of Minnesota Press, 1980), p. 172.

24. E. Warwick Slinn, *Browning and the Fictions of Identity* (London: Macmillan, 1982), p. 17.

NOTES

25. Herbert F. Tucker Jr., 'Dramatic monologue and the overhearing of lyric', in Chaviva Hošek and Patricia Parker, eds., *Lyric Poetry: Beyond New Criticism* (Ithaca, NY: Cornell University Press, 1985), p. 271.

26. Michael Mason, 'Browning and the dramatic monologue', in Isobel Armstrong, ed., *Writers and their Background: Robert Browning* (London: Bell, 1974), pp. 260–5.

27. Preface to *Strafford*, 'Appendix A', *Poetical Works*, ed. Ian Jack and Margaret Smith (Oxford: Clarendon Press, 1984), II, p. 500.

28. George Bornstein, *Poetic Remaking: The Art of Browning, Yeats, and Pound* (University Park, PA: Pennsylvania State University Press, 1988), p. 18. John Lucas makes a similar point when he argues that the 'Cavalier Tunes' are 'jokes at the expense of those contemporaries who believed the way out of England's presumed dark future lay through a retreat into the age of chivalry' (namely, the conservative 'Young England' movement): *England and Englishness: Ideas of Nationhood in English Poetry 1688–1900* (London: Hogarth Press, 1990), p. 169.

29. John Woolford, *Browning the Revisionary* (London: Macmillan, 1988), p. 18.

30. Robert Langbaum, *The Poetry of Experience: The Dramatic Monologue and Modern Literary Tradition*, second edition (Harmondsworth: Penguin, 1974), p. 132. All further references are included in the text. The influence of Langbaum's account has been tremendous, provoking a great deal of debate about the dramatic monologue. For modifications and extensions of his discussion of 'sympathy' and 'judgement', see Christ, *Victorian and Modern Poetics*, pp. 15–52, and A. Dwight Culler, 'Monodrama and the Dramatic Monologue', *PMLA* 90 (1975), pp. 366–75. Alan Sinfield suggests theorising the 'I' of the monologue as a 'feint': 'We experience the "I" of the character in his own right but at the same time sense the author's voice through him': *Dramatic Monologue* (London: Methuen, 1977). Against this trend stands Nina Auerbach, who emphasises the significance of the sceptical auditor or reader either addressed or implied in the poem: 'The dramatic monologue celebrates self-creation, but it is a self-creation enforced by the power of scepticism over the insecurity of being. Other listeners would probably dictate other poems. In its essence, the dramatic monologue asks of us neither sympathy nor judgement. Rather, it strikes home to us the impurity of our own tale telling, the ways in which our own truth has been adjusted, not to a remote and acquiescent audience, but to our intimates who do not believe us': 'Robert Browning's Last Word', *Victorian Poetry*, 22 (1984), p. 167. For a parallel emphasis on the role of the auditor in Victorian poetry, see Dorothy Mermin, *The Audience in the Poem: Five Victorian Poets* (New Brunswick, NJ: Rutgers University Press, 1983). Difficulties in theoretical generalisations of the dramatic monologue arise because of the generic instability of the form. Browning's speakers, auditors, and readers or overhearers vary in disposition. My own view is that this kind of poetry was born out of shifts of concern around a self-consciously psychological interest in bourgeois perceptions of the world.

31. Ralph W. Rader, 'The dramatic monologue and related lyric forms', *Critical Inquiry*, 3 (1976), p. 136. Rader follows up his investigation of different categories of dramatic poetry in 'Notes on some structural varieties and various dramatic "I" poems and their theoretical implications', *Victorian Poetry*, 22 (1984), pp. 103–20.

32. B. R. Jerman, 'Browning's witless duke', *PMLA*, 72 (1957), pp. 488–93, and Laurence Perrine, 'Browning's shrewd duke', *PMLA*, 74 (1957), pp. 157–9, both reprinted in Boyd Litzinger and K.L. Knickerbocker, eds., *The Browning Critics* (Lexington, KT: University of Kentucky Press, 1965), pp. 329–42.

33. Tucker, *Browning's Beginnings*, p. 178.

34. Ibid., p. 178.
35. Eric Griffiths, *The Printed Voice of Victorian Poetry* (Oxford: Clarendon Press, 1989), p. 208. This often digressive study never makes its interesting insights about the monologue as a 'printed voice' entirely clear. Griffiths lodges his argument, in part, against the work of Jacques Derrida; his critique of Derrida would appear to be based on a misconstruction of the deconstructive notion of 'writing' (see pp. 48–59).
36. Tucker, *Browning's Beginnings*, p. 182.
37. Loy D. Martin, 'The inside of time: an essay on the dramatic monologue', in Harold Bloom and Adrienne Munich, eds., *Robert Browning: Twentieth-Century Views* (Englewood Cliffs, NJ: Prentice-Hall, 1979), p. 78.
38. Paul de Man, 'The rhetoric of temporality', in *Blindness and Insight: Essays in the Rhetoric of Contemporary Criticism*, second edition (London: Methuen, 1983), p. 213.
39. Lucas, *England and Englishness*, p. 169.
40. [Coventry Patmore], Review of Alfred Tennyson, *Maud and Other Poems*, *Edinburgh Review*, 102 (1855), p. 513.
41. Alan Sinfield, *Alfred Tennyson*, Rereading Literature (Oxford: Basil Blackwell, 1985), p. 19.
42. In his review of *Corn-Law Rhymes*, Fox writes: 'Poetry is not the privilege of class, either in its production or enjoyment. It belongs to humanity': 'The Poor and Their Poetry', *Monthly Repository*, NS 7 (1832), pp. 189–90. Fox was, however, creating a psychological theory that would, in spite of himself, contribute to driving of poetry away from the concerns of the working classes.
43. H. S. Salt, ed., *Songs of Freedom* (London: Walter Scott, 1893), p. xxi.
44. Patrick Brantlinger, *The Spirit of Reform: British Literature and Politics, 1832–1867* (Cambridge, MA: Harvard University Press, 1975), p. 171. On 22 October 1845 Elizabeth Barrett informed Browning: 'The end you have put to "England in Italy" [the original title of "The Englishman in Italy"] gives unity to the whole . . . just what the poem wanted': *The Letters of Robert Browning and Elizabeth Barrett Barrett 1845–46*, ed. Elvan Kintner, 2 vols (Cambridge, MA: Harvard University Press, 1969), I, p. 244.
45. Lucas writes: 'In sharp contrast to [Matthew] Arnold, Browning constantly denies the authority of any one point of view. He unfixes certainty . . . This essentially democratic strategy is repeatedly used in *Men and Women*': *England and Englishness*, p. 195.

Chapter 3

1. J. Hillis Miller, *The Disappearance of God: Five Nineteenth-Century Writers* (Cambridge, MA: The Belknap Press of Harvard University Press, 1963), p. 108.
2. Peter Allen Dale, *The Victorian Critic and the Idea of History: Carlyle, Arnold, Pater* (Cambridge, MA: Harvard University Press, 1977), p. 4. Among the most significant studies of the representational forms of nineteenth-century historiography is Hayden White, *Metahistory* (Baltimore, MD: Johns Hopkins University Press, 1973).
3. Entry for 10 June 1888 in William Allingham, *A Diary, 1824–1889*, eds. H. Allingham and D. Radford ((1907) London: Penguin Books, 1985), p. 373. Darwin was certainly troubling Browning in old age, as lines from 'With Francis Furini' (1887) indicate:

'I at the bottom, Evolutionists,
Advise beginning, rather. I profess
To know just one fact – my self-consciousness, –
'Twixt ignorance and ignorance enisled, –
Knowledge: before was my Cause – that's styled
God: after, in due course succeeds the rest, –
All that knowledge comprehends – at best –
At worst, conceives about in mild despair.
(349–56)

4. 'To F. J. Furnivall', 11 October 1881, *Browning's Trumpeter: The Correspondence of Robert Browning and Frederick J. Furnivall, 1872–1889*, ed. William S. Peterson (Washington, DC: Decature House Press, 1979), p. 34.
5. See, for example, 'On the Mythical Interpretation of the Bible, from Jahn's Biblical Archaeology', *Monthly Repository*, NS 1 (1827), pp. 633–40.
6. On the relations between 'Bishop Blougram's Apology' and mid-Victorian debates about the Catholic hierarchy, see Julia Markus, 'Bishop Blougram and the literary men', *Victorian Studies*, 21 (1978), pp. 171–95.
7. John Stuart Mill, 'The Spirit of the Age', *Examiner*, 9 January 1831, p. 31 in *Newspaper Writings: December 1822–July 1831*, eds. Ann P. Robson and John M. Robson (Toronto: University of Toronto Press, 1986), p. 228.
8. William Clyde DeVane, *A Browning Handbook*, second edition (New York: Appleton-Century-Crofts, 1955); Mrs [Alexandra] Sutherland Orr, *A Handbook to the Works of Robert Browning*, sixth edition (London: Bell, 1902); *Browning's Sordello*, ed. A.J. Whyte (London: Dent, 1913); and *The Poetical Works of Robert Browning*, II, eds. Ian Jack and Margaret Smith (Oxford: Clarendon Press, 1984). The most comprehensive critical analysis of *Sordello* is David E. Latané, *Browning's Sordello and the Aesthetics of Difficulty*, ELS Monograph Series (Victoria, Canada: University of Victoria, 1987).
9. Thomas Carlyle, 'On History' in *Critical and Miscellaneous Essays, Complete Works*, 30 vols (London: Chapman and Hall, 1896–9), II, pp. 88–9.
10. Mary Ellis Gibson, *History and the Prism of Art: Browning's Poetic Experiments* (Columbus, OH: Ohio State University Press, 1987), p. 3.
11. Carol T. Christ, *Victorian and Modern Poetics* (Chicago, IL: University of Chicago Press, 1984), pp. 112–13.
12. Leonée Ormond, 'Browning and Painting' in Isobel Armstrong, ed., *Writers and Their Work: Robert Browning* (London: Bell, 1974), p. 185.
13. Dante Gabriel Rossetti, 'To William Allingham', 8 January 1856, in 'Letters of D.G. Rossetti', *The Atlantic Monthly*, 78 (1896), pp. 45–9, in Boyd Litzinger and Donald Smalley, eds., *Browning: The Critical Heritage* (London: Routledge and Kegan Paul, 1970), p. 183.
14. In the 1840s and 1850s, an immense number of sources on Italian Renaissance art were available to Browning's hand. Many of these are mentioned in his correspondence, and, apart from Vasari, include Mary Shelley, *Rambles in Germany and Italy in 1840, 1842 and 1843*, 2 vols (London, 1844).
15. J. B. Bullen, 'Browning's "Pictor Ignotus" and Vasari's "Life of Fra Bartlommeo di San Marco', *Review of English Studies*, NS 33 (1972), pp. 313–19. This essay led to an instructive exchange of views about the use and abuse of sources: see Michael H. Bright, 'Browning's Celebrated Pictor Ignotus', *English Language Notes*, 13 (1975–6), pp. 192–4; J. B. Bullen, 'Fra Bartolommeo's Quest for Obscurity',

NOTES

English Language Notes, 13 (1975–6), pp. 206–9; and Michael H. Bright, 'A Reply to J. B. Bullen's "Fra Bartolommeo's Quest for Obscurity', *English Language Notes*, 13 (1975–6), pp. 209–15.

16. Ormond notes that lines 31–3, concerning the painter's dream of public success ('Flowers cast upon the car which bore the freight [a painting], / Through old streets named afresh from the event') resembles an incident in Vasari's life of Cimabue where the Rucellai Madonna was wheeled through the streets to applause: 'Browning and Painting', pp. 195–6.

17. Mrs [Anna] Jameson, *Memoirs of the Early Italian Painters and the Progress of Painting in Italy*, 2 vols (London: Charles Knight, 1845), I, pp. 113–14.

18. A. Dwight Culler, *The Victorian Mirror of History* (New Haven, CT: Yale University Press, 1985), p. 211.

19. Jameson, *Memoirs of the Early Italian Painters*, I, p. 107.

20. Culler, *The Mirror of Victorian History*, p. 213.

21. David J. DeLaura, 'The Context of Browning's Painter Poems: Aesthetics, Polemics, Historics', *PMLA*, 90 (1980), p. 380.

22. Ibid, p. 381.

23. Jameson, *Memoirs of the Early Italian Painters*, I, p. 119.

24. See Johnstone Parr, 'Browning's "Fra Lippo Lippi", Baldinucci, and the Milanesi Edition of Vasari', *English Language Notes*, 3 (1965–6), pp. 197–201; and 'Browning's "Fra Lippo Lippi", Vasari, Masaccio, and Mrs Jameson', *English Language Notes*, 5 (1967–8), pp. 277–83.

25. Edward Dowden drew Browning's attention to several errors in *Men and Women*. Dowden held the first Chair in English at Trinity College, Dublin, and published a number of essays on Browning's poetry, culminating in a monograph in 1904. In October 1866 Dowden received this reply from the poet:

> The first blunder you point out is enormous – only explicable to myself – and hardly that – from the circumstances under which I well remember having written the poem, *Transcendentalism*. I was three parts thro' it, when called to assist a servant to whom a strange accident, partly serious, partly ludicrous, had suddenly happened; and after a quarter of an hour's agitation, of a varied kind, I went back to my room and finished what I begun. I have never touched the piece since, and really suppose that the putting 'Swedish' for 'German' or 'Goerlitzist', is attributable to just that – for I knew something of Boehme, and his autobiography, and how he lived mainly, and died in the Goerlitz where he was born. But the thought in my head was of that revelation he describes, not of his nationality; hence, I hope, my blunder – and such excuse as it may admit of. Depend on it, I will alter the word in the next edition, ay, and look more warily after what may be other slips of the kind.
>
> But, here I get up from my knee and assure you there is no slip in the other case; at least, I was wide awake when I made Fra Lippo the elder practitioner of Art, if not, as I believe, the earlier born. I looked into the matter carefully long ago, and long before I thought of my own poem, from my interest in the Brancacci frescos, indeed in all early Florentine art. I believe the strange confusions and mistakes of Vasari are set tolerably right now: you may know, he took Lippino the son for Lippo the father. I suppose Lippo to have been born, as Baldinucci says, about 1400. He entered the Carmine aged eight years and immediately 'in cambio di studiare, non faceva altro che imbrettare con fantocci i libri' ['Instead of studying, he did nothing but spoil his books with scribbling

faces in them']. Let us assume even, with the last Edition of Vasari, that he was born in 1412, and that this entrance took place in 1420; still, since it is certain that Masaccio did not begin the paintings in the Brancacci before 1440, you see there was a good score of years wherein Lippo might well work and Masaccio watch him working. The Editor sums up 'Se le pitture del Chiostro e della Chiesa del Carine furono fatte da Lippo quando vestiva l'abito Camelitano, bisognerebee conghietturare con ragione che le pitture sue furono poi e studiate e imitate da Masaccio' ['If the paintings in the Cloister and Church of the Carmine were done by Lippo, while he still remained a Carmelite, it would be only reasonable to infer that these paintings were later studied and copied by Masaccio'] – which is my own reasonable conjecture. Masaccio was born in 1402, and, as Vasari writes in his life, 'lavorava nel Carmine seguitando sempre le vestigie di Filippo' ['He worked at the Carmine, always following the steps of Filippo']. But all that 'Life' is a tissue of errors. I could never have had *these* facts shaken out of my head, even by the crying and laughing of poor W. my servant afore mentioned.

Later editions of *Men and Women* altered the offending 'Swedish' to 'German'. But admitting to changes to 'Fra Lippo Lippi' would have meant radical surgery on the poem. Browning lets the blame rest on sources, and so keeps his poem intact. 'To Edward Dowden', 13 October 1866, *Letters of Robert Browning Collected by Thomas J. Wise*, ed. Thurman L. Hood (New Haven, CT: Yale University Press, 1933), pp. 104–5.

26. Ormond, 'Browning and Painting', pp. 207–8. For *The Coronation of the Virgin*, see plate 6 in the same volume.
27. Georgio Vasari, *Lives of the Most Eminent Painters, Sculptors, and Architects*, translated by Mrs Jonathan Foster, 5 vols (London: Henry G. Bohn, 1851), III, p. 194.
28. Ibid., p. 206.
29. On the question of the sexual pains and pleasures played out within the economy of artistic production to be found in 'Andrea del Sarto', see Adrienne Donald, 'Coming out of the canon: sadomasochism, male homoeroticism, romanticism', *Yale Journal of Criticism*, 3 (1989), pp. 239–52. My thanks to John Fletcher (University of Warwick) for drawing my attention to this highly original and provocative essay.
30. Matthew Arnold, 'Preface to the First Edition of *Poems*' (1853) in *Arnold: The Complete Poems*, second edition, eds. Kenneth Allott and Miriam Allott (London: Longman, 1979), p. 655–6.
31. A. Dwight Culler, *Imaginative Reason: The Poetry of Matthew Arnold* (New Haven, CT: Yale University Press, 1966), p. 161.
32. Arnold, 'Preface to the First Edition of *Poems*', pp. 657–68. Subsequent quotations are taken from pp. 662–3 and 670. The review he cites is by David Masson, 'Theories of the poet and a new poet', *North British Review*, 19 (1853), p. 338. An extract from this important discussion of mid-Victorian poetry is reprinted in Isobel Armstrong, *Victorian Scrutinies: Reviews of Poetry 1830–1870* (London: Athlone Press, 1972), pp. 329–35.
33. Links between the poetry of Arnold and Browning have been explored by the following: DeVane, 'Browning and the spirit of Greece', in Herbert Davis, William Clyde DeVane and R.C. Bald, eds., *Nineteenth-Century Studies* (Ithaca, NY: Cornell University Press, 1940), pp. 179–98; John Coates, 'Two versions of

the problem of the modern intellectual: "Empedocles on Etna" and "Cleon"',
Modern Language Review, 79:4 (1984), pp. 769–82; A.W. Crawford, 'Browning's
"Cleon"', *Journal of English and Germanic Philology*, 26 (1927), pp. 485–90; and
Jane A. McCusker, 'Browning's "Aristophanes' Apology" and Matthew Arnold',
Modern Language Review, 79:4 (1984), pp. 783–96. McCusker shows how passages
of *Aristophanes' Apology* closely correspond with several of Arnold's major critical
essays, notably 'The function of criticism at the present time' (1864). DeLaura
provides an exceptionally detailed analysis of Browning's interrelated responses to
Ruskin and Arnold in the 1850s in 'Ruskin, Arnold and Browning's Grammarian:
"Crowded with Culture"' in John Clubbe and Jerome Meckier, eds., *Victorian
Perspectives: Six Essays* (London: Macmillan, 1989), pp. 68–119.
34. Culler, *Imaginative Reason: The Poetry of Matthew Arnold*, p. 162.
35. Linda H. Peterson, 'Biblical typology and the self-portrait of the poet in Robert
Browning', in George P. Landow, ed., *Approaches to Victorian Autobiography*
(Athens, OH: Ohio University Press, 1979), pp. 249–50.
36. Adrienne Munich, 'Troops of shadows: Browning's Types', in Harold Bloom and
Adrienne Munich, eds., *Robert Browning: A Collection of Critical Essays* (Englewood Cliffs, NJ: Prentice-Hall, 1979), p. 169.
37. Ward Hellstrom, 'Time and type in Browning's "Saul"', *English Literary History*,
33:1 (1966), pp. 370–89.
38. Michael Timko, 'Browning upon Butler; or, Theology in the English Isle',
Criticism, 7 (1965), p. 143.
39. Gillian Beer, *Darwin's Plots: Evolutionary Narrative in Darwin, George Eliot and
Nineteenth-Century Fiction* (London: Routledge and Kegan Paul, 1983), p. 84.
40. Ernest Renan, *The Life of Jesus*, People's Edition (London: Trubner, 1863), p. 289.
41. E.S. Shaffer, 'Browning's St John: The casuistry of the Higher Criticism' in *'Kubla
Khan' and The Fall of Jerusalem: The Mythological School in Biblical Criticism and
Secular Literature, 1770–1880* (Cambridge: Cambridge University Press, 1975), p.
201. Another critical essay worth noting here is Daniel A. Harris, 'The "Figured
Page": Dramatic Epistle in Browning and Yeats', in Richard J. Finneran, ed., *Yeats
Annual No.1* (London: Macmillan, 1982), pp. 133–94.
42. Elizabeth Barrett, 'To Robert Browning', 20 March 1846, *The Letters of Robert
Browning and Elizabeth Barrett Barrett*, ed. Elvan Kintner, 2 vols (Cambridge, MA:
The Belknap Press of Harvard University Press, 1969), p. 43.

Chapter 4

1. 'The Brownings' marriage was, for both of them, not only extremely happy (here
especially the legend does not lie, although it may strain credulity) but also
artistically enabling. A very distinguished feminist poet and critic once asked me
if it were not true that Elizabeth Barrett Browning wrote all her best poetry before
her marriage; no, it is not true – quite the contrary. Being a happy wife and mother
and a prolific and successful poet was her most radical revision [to poetic tradition]
of all': Dorothy Mermin, *Elizabeth Barrett Browning; The Origins of a New Poetry*
(Chicago, IL: University of Chicago Press, 1989), p. 5.
2. Auerbach makes some very provocative points about possible transactions
between the Brownings' poems, particularly her suggestion that in *The Ring and the
Book* Robert 'freed himself to transplant her legend' of *Aurora Leigh* 'into his own
poetic territory': 'Robert Browning's Last Word', *Victorian Poetry*, 22 (1984), p.
168. See also Mary Rose Sullivan, '"Some Interchange of Grace": "Saul" and

Sonnets from the Portuguese', *Browning Institute Studies*, 15 (1987), pp. 55–68.

3. The Brownings' disagreements (and intermittent agreements) about Napoleon III – which were many and varied, depending on the changing political climate – are traced in Flavia Alaya, 'The Ring, the rescue, and the Risorgimento: reunifying the Brownings' Italy', *Browning Institute Studies*, 6 (1978), pp. 1–41. The Brownings were possibly considering publishing a joint volume of poems on Italian politics until Palmerston's Liberal ministry took power in 1860, making redundant Robert Browning's objections to the lack of British intervention in aiding the Italian struggle for freedom.

4. Elizabeth Barrett Browning, 'To Mrs James Martin', 11 December 1851, *The Letters of Elizabeth Barrett Browning*, ed. Frederic G. Kenyon, 2 vols (London: Macmillan, 1897), II, p. 37.

5. Relations between the Brownings and their poetry have so far been explored through examinations of the courtship correspondence: see, in particular, Daniel Karlin, *The Courtship of Robert Browning and Elizabeth Barrett* (Oxford: Clarendon Press, 1985), which is especially sensitive to the complex modulations of feeling in the letters of 1845–6. Lee Erickson considers Barrett Browning's shaping influence on Browning in *Robert Browning: His Poetry and His Audiences* (Ithaca, NY: Cornell University Press, 1984), pp. 104–31.

6. Ann P. Brady, *Pompilia: A Feminist Reading of Robert Browning's* The Ring and the Book (Athens, OH: Ohio University Press, 1988), p. 7.

7. *Robert Browning: The Poems*, eds. John Pettigrew with Thomas J. Collins, 2 vols (Harmondsworth: Penguin, 1981), I, p. 1138.

8. George M. Ridenour assumes the speaker of 'Two in the Campagna' is female: 'a woman speaks of her inability to love completely and constantly the man she addresses': 'Four Modes in the Poetry of Robert Browning', in Harold Bloom and Adrienne Munich, eds., *Robert Browning: Twentieth-Century Views* (Englewood Cliffs, NJ: Prentice Hall, 1979), p. 19.

9. Richard Oastler, 'Yorkshire Slavery', *Leeds Mercury*, 16 October 1830 cited and discussed in Catherine Gallagher, *The Industrial Reformation of English Fiction 1832–1867* (Chicago, IL: University of Chicago Press, 1985), pp. 3–35.

10. John Lucas, *England and Englishness: Ideas of Nationhood in English Poetry 1688–1900* (London: Hogarth Press, 1990), p. 193.

11. Barrett Browning, 'To Sarianna Browning', 12 June 1855, *The Letters of Elizabeth Barrett Browning*, II, p. 203.

12. Isobel Armstrong, 'Browning and Victorian poetry of sexual love', in Isobel Armstrong, ed., *Writers and their Background: Robert Browning* (London: Bell, 1974), pp. 290–1.

13. Roy E. Gridley, *The Brownings and France: A Chronicle with Commentary* (London: Athlone Press, 1982), p. 108.

14. Patricia Thomson, *George Sand and the Victorians: Her Reputation and Influence in Nineteenth-Century England* (London: Macmillan, 1977), p. 56.

15. Adelaide Anne Procter, *Legends and Lyrics and Other Poems* (1858; London: Dent, nd), p. 254. In the late 1850s, Procter became involved in the Langham Place group, the first highly organised group of feminist campaigners in Britain. For several years Procter worked as Secretary to the Society for the Promotion of the Employment of Women. Her father, 'Barry Cornwall' (Bryan Waller Procter), was well known to Browning, since both men moved in circles close to Dickens.

16. 'To Julia Wedgwood', *Robert Browning and Julia Wedgwood: A Broken Friendship as Revealed in their Letters*, ed. Richard Curle (London: John Murray and Jonathan

NOTES

Cape, 1937), p. 123. It is worth noting in passing that Wedgwood, in the last of her published letters to Browning, remarks: 'You know you owe us an adequate translation of what your wife was to you' (p. 205) – something he never offered to the reading public.

17. Charles Dickens, *Hard Times: For These Times* (1854; Harmondsworth: Penguin, 1969), pp. 102–3.

18. Brady, *Pompilia: A Feminist Reading of Robert Browning's* The Ring and the Book, p. 133.

19. Richard D. Altick and James F. Loucks II, *Browning's Roman Murder Story* (Chicago, IL: University of Chicago Press, 1968), p. 57. William E. Buckler argues energetically against Altick and Loucks's study, and Sullivan, *Browning's Voices in 'The Ring and the Book'* (Toronto: University of Toronto Press, 1969): see *Poetry and Truth in Robert Browning's* The Ring and the Book (New York: New York University Press, 1985).

Chronology

1812	Browning born in Camberwell, south London, 12 May.
1824	Completes first collection of poems, *Incondita*, and shows them to W. J. Fox. Poems subsequently burned. Two of these poems survive, having been copied into an album book by Sarah Flower.
1828	Attends University College, London for one term.
1833	*Pauline; A Fragment of a Confession* (published anonymously).
1835	*Paracelsus.*
1837	*Strafford.*
1838	First visit to Italy.
1840	*Sordello.*
1841	*Bells and Pomegranates* I: *Pippa Passes.*
1842	*Bells and Pomegranates* II: *King Victor and King Charles. Bells and Pomegranates* III: *Dramatic Lyrics.*

1843	*Bells and Pomegranates* IV: *The Return of the Druses*. *Bells and Pomegranates* V: *A Blot in the 'Scutcheon*.
1844	*Bells and Pomegranates* VI: *Colombe's Birthday*. Visits Italy.
1845	First letter to Elizabeth Barrett, 10 January. *Bells and Pomegranates* VII: *Dramatic Romances and Lyrics*.
1846	*Bells and Pomegranates* VIII: *Luria* and *A Soul's Tragedy*. Marriage to Elizabeth Barrett. 19 September: departure for Pisa.
1847	Move to Florence.
1849	*Poems* (two volumes). Robert Wiedemann Barrett Browning born.
1850	*Christmas-Eve and Easter-Day*.
1852	'Essay on Shelley'.
1855	*Men and Women*.
1861	Death of Elizabeth Barrett Browning. Return to London.
1863	*The Poetical Works* (three volumes).
1864	*Dramatis Personae*.
1868	*The Poetical Works* (six volumes).
1868–69	*The Ring and the Book*.
1871	*Balaustion's Adventure*; *Prince Hohenstiel-Schwangau*.
1872	*Fifine at the Fair*.
1873	*Red Cotton Night-Cap Country*.
1875	*Aristophanes' Apology*; *The Inn Album*.
1876	*Pacchiarotto and How He Worked in Distemper*.
1877	Translation of *The Agamemnon of Aeschylus*.
1878	*La Saisiaz: Two Poets of Croisic*.
1879	*Dramatic Idyls*.
1880	*Dramatic Idyls: Second Series*.
1881	Browning Society founded in London.
1882	D.C.L. from University of Oxford.

1883	*Jocoseria.*
1884	LLD from University of Edinburgh. *Ferishtah's Fancies.*
1887	*Parleyings with Certain People of Importance in Their Day.*
1888–89	*The Poetical Works* (sixteen volumes).
1889	*Asolando,* 12 December; Browning dies at Venice later that day. Buried in Westminster Abbey.

Suggestions for Further Reading

Bibliography: Philip Drew, ed., *Robert Browning: An Annotated Bibliography of Criticism* (Hemel Hempstead: Harvester Wheatsheaf, 1990). The journal, *Victorian Poetry*, carries an annual overview of current Browning studies. **Biography**: A definitive biography is still awaited. Several biographies are available, mostly repeating the same information. The best one to date is still Betty Miller, *Robert Browning: A Portrait* (London: John Murray, 1952) – well informed, witty, speculative, but not altogether accurate. John Maynard's very detailed *Browning's Youth* (Cambridge, MA: Harvard University Press, 1977) is an indispensable tool of research for the early years. **Letters**: Various collections of Browning's letters have been collected since his death in 1889. *The Brownings' Correspondence*, edited by Philip Kelley and Ronald Hudson (Winfield, KA: Wedgestone Press; London: Athlone Press) has, at the time of writing, reached the seventh of its projected forty volumes. It is a masterwork of scholarship, and helpfully includes as many contemporary reviews of the Brownings' books as possible. Daniel Karlin has made a useful selection of the Brownings' love letters: *Robert Browning and Elizabeth Barrett: The Courtship Correspondence 1845–46* (Oxford: Oxford University Press, 1989). **Criticism**: William Clyde DeVane's *Handbook* to Browning's work helps to clear up obscurities: see the second edition (New York: Appleton-Century-Crofts, 1955). Many of the most useful studies – especially outstanding individual essays in periodicals – are mentioned in the footnotes to the preceding chapters, and are too numerous to list again here. Perhaps the most stimulating study in recent years is Herbert F. Tucker, *Browning's Beginnings: The Art of Disclosure* (Minneapolis, MN: University of Minnesota

Press, 1980), although it pays scant attention to the historical and cultural contexts of Browning's work. A strong collection of articles has been edited by Harold Bloom and Adrienne Munich: *Robert Browning: Twentieth-Century Views* (Englewood Cliffs, NJ: Prentice Hall, 1979). A more traditional and equally informative collection, reflecting British critical approaches of the 1970s, is Isobel Armstrong, ed., *Writers and Their Background* (London: Bell, 1974). Commentary on Browning's writing appears, of course, in many general studies of Victorian poetry. In relation to Victorian debates about Victorian poetry, see Isobel Armstrong, *Victorian Scrutinies: Reviews of Poetry 1830–1870* (London: Athlone Press, 1972). Browning's place within poetic tradition is examined in Carol T. Christ, *Victorian and Modern Poetics* (Chicago, IL: University of Chicago Press, 1984). His distinctly Victorian concern with history and history writing is considered in A. Dwight Culler, *The Victorian Mirror of History* (New Haven, CT: Yale University Press, 1985).

Index

INDEX

INDEX